Musings of the Mind

DURING CORONA TIMES

Musings of the Mind

DURING CORONA TIMES

LALIT MENGI

PRABHAT PAPERBACKS

Published by

PRABHAT PAPERBACKS

An Imprint of Prabhat Prakashan Pvt. Ltd.
4/19 Asaf Ali Road,
New Delhi–110 002 (INDIA)
e-mail: prabhatbooks@gmail.com

ISBN 978-93-5521-316-7
MUSINGS OF THE MIND DURING CORONA TIMES
by Lalit Mengi

Edition
2022

Price
₹ 250 (Rupees Two Hundred Fifty Only)

Printed at
Sanjay Printer Sahibabad

Preface

Writing has been my obsession;
With an urge to read, learn and for expression.

Many a time, I would reverie;
If I could give my thoughts a formal shape ever.

Reluctance, lack of confidence, kept me at bay;
I would wonder, in the cherished realms, I would stray;
But till I am firm enough, let me be away.

With Covid times and concomitant solitude,
came calling opportunity, knocking at my door.
Confined to my groove, away from multitudes;
Writing becoming a regular story, staying indoors.
I read and re-read books, with a lot of gratitude;
To the great authors, triggering my dormant instincts,
to the highest magnitude.

My good friends spurred me into action;
Not to look behind, their nudge I can't but mention.

Gradually picking up subjects, contemporary and
general at random;

Many a time, ideas and thoughts would languidly linger;
Sometimes, I would draw a blank, but with crossed fingers;
Thank God, the flood gates did open
and this task I undertook, not to abandon.

Breaching the bounds of initial trepidations of its kind,
shunning trivia of the daily grind;
I would dedicate hours on end;
Catching up with the theme, with a focused mind;
Slowly and gradually, commitment with patience did descend.

I kept writing, weaving my stray thoughts into a book;
To the best of my ability, I present to you, my esteemed
readers, for your scrutiny and views;
Discrepancy if any be, brought to my notice if you can,
and I be excused;
Maiden attempt it is, and genuine efforts it took.

In my twilight years, amidst the gleams and slumber;
Dreams and ambitions yet alive, I wonder;
To my sedulous yearning and humble effort, I do surrender;
To seek what I know not, but to get a pedestal to my
musings, nothing more nothing under.

❑

Introduction

Writing has been my passion, beginning the journey right from the school days, with essays of the curriculum, with an ever increasing impulse to broaden the scope and expression, as I went along stage to stage, on the canvas of times.

During my service career as a civil engineer, my writing essentially was concentrated on technical subjects, yet it didn't prevent me and my innate proclivities, to remain abreast with the contemporary events, and to pen down my thoughts off and on.

Post retirement, with all the time at my disposal, the urge to write gained further momentum. But it remained largely focused on the presentation of technical papers, in the Institution of Engineers. I did get due recognition in the process, yet it was falling short of my goals. Somehow there remained an inexplicable reluctance on my part, to give an outlet to my thoughts, in the shape of a book.

The outbreak of the pandemic in early 2020, afforded an opportunity, though in adversity, amidst our lives going topsy-turvy, and in forced solitude. I started writing regularly tracking the journey of COVID-19, its fall out and the transformation in our lives as a sequel and sharing on electronic media. Unconsciously my style of writing became prose in poetry, generally concluding with befitting couplets of Urdu poetry. I was buoyed by the inspiring comments of my friends, who genuinely prompted me to consolidate my thoughts and take it to the next level. This is how exactly my book project took off.

While covering COVID-19, which has wrought havoc on humanity, I have tried to bring out in the backdrop of our upended lives, human traits and behaviour, trepidations and tribulations, strengths and frailties of humanity. Besides I have dealt with subjects of day-to-day life, of the normal times, across a wide spectrum, with many of abstract nature, right from the mundane to the metaphysical level. As I kept on writing, in the style, I mentioned above, did I realize that it has opened new windows, stretching my imagination to astronomical heights. Like an artist, who plays with his brush and paint, to create a work of art with his imaginative skills, poetic expression is no less, with a profound ingenuity let loose by the unexplored territories, of the human mind. A cornucopia of ideas started flowing, transcending the ordinary domain of thoughts, seeking new vistas, which had eluded me so far. This transformation was triggered by the complete works of William Shakespeare, I had read many times over, and lately Vikram Seth's amazing Golden Gate in 281 sonnets, besides poems of great poets like Lord Alfred Tennyson, Khalil Gibran, William Wordsworth, T.S. Eliot, Lord Byron and John Milton. To fully understand the structures, forms and styles, I practically had to dig in my heels, spending hours searching on various websites. Firstly, it was to cover the journey of poetry, having chosen this as a cherished subject of one of my write-ups, and secondly, to decipher the metric lines, and appreciate the rhythm and rhymes. I have earnestly tried to maintain the format of my writings, in poetic expression. In my heart of hearts, I do wish to try my hands, on absolute poetry in iambs and in pentameters, at some stage; rather than prose in poetry, when my poetic skills come of age.

In my write-ups, I quite often venture into the coveted realms of great thinkers, philosophers, saints and Yogis, who have spent their lifetimes to understand the enigmatic human life, a beautiful gift of God, yet for average mortals like me, remains a labyrinth, a conundrum. Nevertheless I could peep into some aspects, and the veil did lift a bit, going through treasured writings of the extraordinary authors and exalted souls like Dr. S. Radhakrishnan, Paramhansa Yogananda, and Sri Aurobindo. Above all Rabindranath Tagore's Gitanjali, a collection of highly inspirational poems, devoted to the universal Lord, did leave an indelible imprint in my mind. My journey was further facilitated, by my in-depth study of poetry as I mentioned above, along with subject music amongst others, so closely related. The two together, in tandem, with musical notes nudged me into the cherished territories, normally beyond my reach. Poetry and music are wonderful tools to relate; to the life's philosophy, its nuances and tales; what otherwise, would require volumes to narrate.

❑

Acknowledgements

"Musings of the Mind-During Corona Times" though authored by me, is indeed a conjunctive effort of my family along with me, if I am fair enough to avow. All through amidst the peaks and troughs of the immense task; the prompt feedback and unbiased comments from both my son Vikram and daughter Deepika, spurred me keeping up the stream of my thoughts intact. My brother and sister too, with whom I shared few write-ups on the nostalgic yesteryears, were gracious enough to appreciate the reflection of the decades gone by, assisting me as well tracking the chronicles of time. Not far behind was my nephew Sunil, who having authored a book, was an immense help with his fair critique comments and suggestions. Most importantly, it was my daughter's painstaking total review of the manuscript that helped me, winnow the writings and bring the final draft to fruition.

I deeply appreciate the invaluable contribution of Sidharth and Sushil, who are both like family members to me, of undertaking the onerous job of bringing my work to digital format. My acknowledgement is also due to my cousin, Major General Purshotam Vig, AVSM, VSM (Retd) who is my childhood friend as well, by inspiring me through his prolific writings, having seven books to his credit, across a wide spectrum, from his distinguished military career to philosophy of life, in various formats including poetry. All in all, I stand in deep gratitude to my family, for making my job lot easier with their direct and indirect support. I am beholden to my several "Facebook" friends like, Hafiz Mirza, S.Amarjeet Singh Bedi, Kesar Salalia, Dr. Satish Gupte, Devinder Sharma, and my batch mates Dr. Sudesh Spolia and Dr. Raj Abrol for their encouraging comments on my posts, prompting me to expand the scope of my writings. But above all, it was Dr. Raj Abrol's persistent nudge to let me give my thoughts an outlet by way of a book, which set the ball rolling, to undertake the project. I take this opportunity as well to extend my profound gratitude to Mr. K. B. Jandial IAS (Retd), ex-member of JKPSC, political analyst, columnist, a man of letters, for his highly inspirational words of appreciation on some of my write-ups I shared with him, which bolstered my confidence and I was all revved up in my mission.

I am indebted to internet, Google, and web media, which offered an extravaganza of information on various topics. Many a time it comes to my mind that the day begins and ends with a Google search. I fondly recall pertinent observation made by late Dr. A.P.J. Abdul Kalam, ex president of India, in a function at Shri Mata Vaishno Devi University Katra (J&K) that it will not be the availability but the management of knowledge that will govern the 21st century.

My grateful thanks are due to the publishers and their team of editors to fine tune, design and give pleasing shape to my book. I appreciate their patience, for coordinating and bearing with my requirements. Overall it has been a fascinating journey from the thoughts germinating in the mind, terminating into a book, to me a dream project of its kind.

The last thing that comes to my mind, to unwind;
As I conclude offering acknowledgements;
Is that though, thoughts were mine, yet effort was combined;
Of so many hands behind, who deserve profuse compliments.

❑

Contents

CHAPTER 1

PHILOSOPHY OF LIFE—AN INSIGHT

1.

"Queue"

At the post office, stood I in a queue,
To draw quarterly interest, as earlier I would do;
This time, the task felt onerous, my restlessness grew,
The queue hardly moved, though in front of me were few:
I wondered, whether the computer was slow or the hand on it was new,
Finally reached the counter, when I was due.

A disarming smile greeting me, soothing my frayed nerves;
Assuring me, despite the work load the system serves:
More so during corona times, with abated verve;
With safety norms in place, better understanding, it deserves.

Back home, my stray thoughts transport me to the daily wagers' queues;
Who after a hard day's toil stand patiently, to collect their dues.

Queuing up is a way of life;

At the Railway station, Airport terminal,
bus terminal, travelling by any mode;

Everyone in hurry, some to board and some to deboard:

So be, at the places of worship, tourist
resorts and department stores;

At the Malls, Banks, Theatres, Hospitals and many more,

Occasions joyous or stressful, of delight or strife.

In the weddings, buffets', common sight it is seeing
people queuing with their plates;

Health conscious with frugal helpings,
satisfying their palate.

Amidst the joyous moods, to justify the wide range of
food, don't mind a full platter;

And the ravenous, leaving no opportunity,
yield to rapacious instincts to satiate.

When we look at the extravaganza and wasted food,
the bountiful events offer;

One wonders, how can we be insensitive and forget,

The destitute, who queue up for a morsel,
to their fate's regret:

Shouldn't we limit the cuisines and instead
to the needy, food and help proffer?

"Queue"

There is another queue, where no one has to stand;

Metaphysically it exists, across the spectrum of mortals, irrespective of any brand;

Where no one would conjure to be ever there, but be the last, with no demand;

In the wretched state of the worst kind though, yet to withstand.

The strands, out of human reach, destiny would weave and understand;

The last journey from the world, where and when, we wish we could pre-plan.

Befitting couplet of legendary poet Zauq, hitting the nail on the head:

Ho umre-khizr bhi tau ho maalum, waqt-e-marg,
Hum kya rahe yahan, abhi aayai, abhi chale,

Meaning: Even if given Khizr's life, we will but complain; A while ago here we came, in another while we go.

Khizr: Name of a prophet, who is said to have discovered the fountain of life and drank it.

Laai hyat aayai, qaza le chali chale,
Apni Khushi na aayai, na apni khushi chale.

Meaning: Commissioned by life we come, commanded by death we go.

Hyat: Life; existence

Qaza: Death

Transcending the entire queues', there is yet one queue; of human imagination, the ultimate goal one seeks;

To merge with the all-pervasive Brahman,
when the urge peaks.

Looking for the benevolent glance, I too wish
to be in the divine queue.

Legendary poet Ghalib's couplet says it all:

Partawai Khur se hai shabnam ko fana ki taalim,
Main bhi hun, ek inaait ki nazar hone tak.

Meaning: The reflection of the sun, heralds the dew-drop's doom;

I too await your kindly glance.

❑

The Urdu couplets and translation is from K.C. Kanda's books on Urdu poetry.

2.

"Surrender to the One and One only" — An Insight

As a result of prolonged confinement due to COVID-19, aloofness indeed proved so fruitful. Away from the humdrum of life, in the cozy environs of the house, with serenity all around, solitude did trigger a strong desire lying dormant, to explore the inner realms. Giving expression, surrendering to the one and one only the Almighty, in the following words;

When our spirits soar high;

Everything going hunky-dory, our ambitions may fly;

Sometime on cloud nine, sometime over the moon, yet lurking fear remains close by.

God never promised always blue sky[1];

Sometime it may be sunny, sometimes rainy; other times may be dry.

God never promised flower studded pathways, luxuriant lifestyle;

In the seventh heaven, all the while!

Therefore remain grounded deep inside,
even when you tend to fly:

Knowing not, when a bad patch of destiny, from
nowhere will descend and upend our lives.

A beautiful gift of God though, life is enigmatic, a
labyrinth, yet we have to live;

With its ups and downs, rather than like a treadmill,
good to be with a mind still.

Discard the false garb; be real and genuine to the core;
Wearing the armour of truthfulness,
let our actions be, with sincerity galore;

Let's be a karamyogi of substance, bringing
our best attributes to the fore.

Good to surrender not reluctantly but fully right from the
youthful days, when the life is on prime;
To the one and one only, master of the universe, with
profound gratitude, making our lives sublime.

Let's be instinctively cheerful, exultant at times, yet with a
balanced mind not to go overboard;

When the fate changes track, becomes easier, from the
happy journey to deboard.

Some beautiful couplets of Urdu poetry by Dag on the subject:

Sabak aisa parha diya tune;

Dil se sub kuch mita diya tu ne.

Lakh dene ka ek dena hai;

Dil-e-be-muda diya tu ne.

Mit gayai dil se naqsh-e-baatil sab;

Naqsha apna jama diya tu ne.

Dag ko koun dene wala tha;

Jo diya, aai khuda diya tu ne.

Dil-e-be-muda; Meaning contented heart

Naqsh-e-baatil; Meaning false imprints.

❑

Adapted from my Facebook post of 18th October, 2020.

Urdu poetry is from K.C. Kanda's book On Urdu Ghazalas An Anthology.

[1]This line, and the inspiration is from the book "Wings of Fire" by the revered ex-president of India, Dr A. P. J. Abdul Kalam.

3.

"Never Too Late"

I couldn't say, what I had to say;
Maybe, fallen prey to levity of times:
Or was it reluctance of the balking mind;
Delayed to rewind, till I was grey.

Yet let me say, with each passing day;
Ideas falling in line, riding on cloud nine.
Childlike innocence, transporting me to prime;
To stray into fond vistas, there is yet leeway.

The day I compose a poem, limitless is my pleasure;
To recompense my wasted hours, at me gnawing:
To write, insatiable gets my appetite, to measure;
Yet at times, a drought of ideas not withstanding.

In all my humility, I am amazed;
Transcending the boundaries of constraints:
Seeing my thoughts burgeoning at a rapid pace;
Keeping at bay, age and psychological restraints.

As I get along, to accomplish what I can;
My conviction gets strong, whatsoever the stage:
You say, when you can, unplanned or planned;
Many a times lying dormant, your skills remain caged.

Let's make a humble beginning, hang you on;
Slowly and gradually to reach, where you belong:
With consistent efforts and clarity, may not take too long.

4.
Human Mind — An Enigma

Human mind, through faculties, like thought,
imagination, memory, will and sensation;
Exhibits its presence, triggering mental manifestation,
like pain, perception:
Like experience, belief, desire, and emotion to mention;
There being many theories of the mind and its functions.

Earliest recorded works on the mind were brought to fore,
By the scholars of yore, like Zarathushtra,
The Buddha, Plato, Aristotle,
Adi Shankra, and many more;
Greek and Indian philosophers, expanding
its size and scope.

Modern scientific knowledge treats the mind,
a product of brain,
Its conscious and unconscious aspects;

Nevertheless, which attributes do contribute,
and their prospects;
With two schools of thoughts, debatable they remain.
One, viewing intellectual functions,
like reasoning and memory constituting mind,

Emotions subjective in nature, like love, hate, joy and fear,
Of its kind, to be seen different from mind:

The other arguing, rational and emotional both to be,
but inseparable and near.

In popular usage, mind is synonymous
with human thought,
In our private conversations with it;
Sometime relaxed, sometime tight we sit:
Eagerly wait for the answers, we besought.

We make up our minds, change our minds,
Sometimes in two minds, goes on all the time.
Intrinsically too, we exhibit myriad traits;
Others' emotions we sometime exacerbate,
and sometime placate.

Be that as it may, I take fancy to say
On this tricky subject in my way;

Not to trivialize the supremacy of the supercomputer;

But on lighter note, may I communicate with my mind,
my tutor, troublemaker, as well as troubleshooter.

The day begins and ends, understanding
you and your guiles,

Being your vassal, bound to bear with your leisure;

Remain I on tenterhooks, all the while:

Not to defy, but to satiate you and your pleasures.

To your moods bow I, fake happiness I pretend,

Conjure your benevolence, to let me breathe:

With riders none, at my ease;

Let me have my will, my discretions to tend.

Surrendering my sovereign rights to you,
lowering my stature,

Was I a naïve, to let you be my master,
rather than my slave?

In my own eyes, become I my own image's caricature;

How I wish, I could but retrieve my identity, now at stake.

One moment on the seventh heaven, other moment
over the coals, look I besieged,

By the tantrums, you play upon me;

Whether to ignore or to hear you all the more,
as you command me to be:

Knowing not how to react, I am intrigued.

So often you put breaks, in my scheme of things,
As if by arrows and slings, by your vacillating instincts;
Hedge me in my tracks, to me it seems;
As if playing spoilsport, in my cherished dreams.

As I silently protest, yet am aware,
It's a no-brainer, the favour I seek;
Herculean task it is, as difficult as easy to beseech,
Of you, to rein in whom, holy men spent lifetimes,
away from public glare.
In all my humility, let practical be me;
Let better sense prevail upon me.

Tossed upon waves, on the wheels of time;

Having seen enough, glitter and glamour leaving behind;

Away from its sway, try I may on a calm pond of life, I pray-

To put all my efforts, to seek divine display.

Living in the materialistic world, yet detached,

To perform duties carrying no remorse;

To righteous deeds, stay attached:

Put aside insinuations, and stick to a balanced course.

Let my spiritual stage, come of age,

Let me presage, tranquillity galore;

With my meditation sessions, let me engage:

Wishing nothing under, nothing more.

Inspired by William Shakespeare's sonnets 57 & 58
For introductory stanzas, accessed https://www.Wikipedia.com

5.

"Harnessing Turbulent Mind" — Exploring Inner Realms

Yogis and sages spent lifetimes to understand the philosophy of life and rein in their minds. We, living in the materialistic world can surely make efforts to balance our lives, transforming discordant notes into harmonious and divine music. Beset by corona, prolonged lockdown and restricted life thereafter, resultant aloofness and solitude, offered an opportunity to explore the inner realms:

Akin to aloofness, stealing upon the
muddled mind, solitude you may beget;

Prolonged detachment, not by choice though,
yet had salutary effect.

Reining in the turbulent mind, a herculean task though,
we need to strive;

In the adversity, here comes an opportunity,
to transform our lives:

Let's jettison the dustbowl of unwanted thoughts;
relieve our souls of the strife.

Retrieve and rejuvenate, weltered in the quagmire of worldly glare, the stormy mind;

Let's harness it; it's time to clean and leave the cobwebs behind:

By workouts, Yog Kriya, Pranayams and meditation, making our lives sublime;

Integrating body, mind and soul, essence of Yoga, devoting available, precious time:

Eternal bliss will descend, beggaring description, of its kind.

The mind in harmony with the intellect, spiritually recharged;

Learn we may, to discern the real and mirage.

Exploring our inner selves is as good as exploring God.

The soul is the self, it is Brahman, it is absolute, and it is ubiquitous residing in us;

Let's rediscover ourselves, transcend the new realms thus.

Legendary poet Mir-taqi-Mir has made beautiful observations on the subject through these couplets:

Hasti apni habab ki si hai;

Yeh namaaish sarab ki si hai

Meaning: Our life is like a water bubble; this pageant show is a vast mirage.

Pahuncha jo aap ko, to pahuncha Khuda ke taeen;

Malum ab Hua, ke bahut mein bhi dur tha.

Meaning: By knowing myself, I have known the Lord; how removed from me, I see, I was.

Tha woh to rashk-e-hur-e-bahishti, hamin mein Mir;

Samjhe na ham, to fahm ka kasoor tha.

Meaning: The beauty envied of Hur, Mir resides within; if we can't see this truth, ours is the fault.

❑

Adapted from my Facebook post of 2nd October, 2020.
Urdu poetry with translation is from "Masterpieces of Urdu Ghazals" by K.C. Kanda.

6.

"Three in One"

Many a time would it occur to me,
do I waste my precious hours?

Lost in the past, at the altar of idle hours;

To dig from the crevices, memories sweet and sour.

Many a time, would it also occur to me,
I may have got it wrong;

The hidden thoughts, getting by the day strong;

Yearning to swell and blossom, and stay long.

For a happy life they say "Live in the present"
an adage to last

Absolutely, yet an insight into your life without the past;

Would end up, half-cooked story, till you part.

Some others would say "stay connected to your roots",
stick to your past.

Yet the journey of life, without present and future,
will go apart.

"Three in One"

A study of religious texts, particularly the Upanishads, did clear the mist,

Of my mind's dilemma and the subject's gist:

Neither should we bask, in the glory of our past;

Imperil it would, our present, at huge cost.

Nor to preclude future, from the domain of our thought;

But to live in harmony, and not get lost.

Let's invoke the sacred symbol AUM[1]*, of completeness and concreteness, trinity in essence;*

Of being, non-being and becoming; birth, life, and death in consonance;

Of Brahma, Vishnu and Shiva; so are the past, present and future, in unison the sum and substance.

❑

[1]The interpretation of the sacred symbol AUM is from "Indian Philosophy Volume 1", by S Radhakrishnan page 185.

7.

"Remembering a Dear Friend"

Night after night of wait, and the dawn
on the look, desperate;
Summers and springs, verdure and blooming flowers,
Bring to the fore, the memories mirthful and sour;
But to alleviate my solitude and distress, and fade.

Your anecdotes, communicative skills, at voluble pace;
Your grace and blitheful face;
Resonate before my mind's eyes:
Alas, now deprived of, I sigh.

To my eloquence, who shall lend his ear?
With whom, shall I, my verse share?
Who would applaud and listen with curiosity rare?
Who would longingly, with alacrity hear?

"Remembering a Dear Friend"

Where did you disappear?

Stealthily changed you, your abode;

How many miles, together we strode:

I sit in the hope, from the skies, you may someday appear.

It may have been some clandestine act,

Even though, to transport you to the higher realms;

To recompense your good deeds, with open arms;

Though depriving your fans, here on the planet earth, of your charms.

I, your bosom friend, am unable to accept the ineluctable fact.

Am I hamstrung in dismay?

Am I a naïve, with nerves frayed?

The reach of divine Kingdom, my banal instincts can't assay.

Destiny and fate, beyond our scope, is laid.

Yet I am, within my right to say,

The precious memories of the worthy times, will always stay;

Like a fresh breeze, in the daily chores, recall as I may;
Wishing you, my dear friend eternal peace, I pray.

❑

8.

"Aim High, Yet Don't Fly"

Listen to your mind's vibes; keep your goals high;
Good times may be knocking at your doors, well nigh:
Why fret and sigh, new sights opening, why not try;
Lest you repent, later in life, it passed you by.

Surely you being within your right, to decide;
Trepidations of the mind, keep aside.

To soar to glorious heights, it's your choice, your life.
No one dare question, your making future bright;
Yet be aware, remain grounded, of your inner self don't lose sight.
With unfeigned humility, in your achievements, do thrive.

Not to forget, fortunes switch sides;
Leave as fast as they arrive;

Without any notice, leave you high and dry.

At the end of the day, what will survive?

Not your wealth, but your goodwill and deeds remain alive.

Drawing inspiration from, couplets of Nikhat Ifthikar's ghazal in a Mushaira:

Shouq ko Aazm-e-Safar rakhiye,

Be-Khabar ban ke, sab khabar rakhiye,

Chahe nazren hon Aasmanon par,

Paaoun lekin Zamin par rakhiye.

Meaning:

Keep your ambition high;

Yet be detached, but fully aware;

Soar you may to the sky;

Yet be grounded, and don't fly.

❑

9.

"Lighten Your Baggage"

With heavy baggage, in the train, sat I tight;
It's safety high on mind, counting the bags many times.
Night arrived, finishing with the meals, of and on I would sleep, with fears high;
In my heart of hearts, cursing myself, why couldn't I travel light?

At home, as I look around,
Do I find, superfluous items and gadgets, of no use;
Yet to part with the clutter, my mind would refuse:
But to be abound with all this stuff, beyond the pale of reason it sounds.

As I look into my wardrobe, apparel and suits,
Seldom used, with no explicable excuse.
Even after dispensing, there are quite a few; I am bemused;

Reminded of the days, when new clothes would be rarely stitched, as better sense would intuit.

Should I seek solace, seeing people hoarding the same way?

No way; we all have to carry our burden of life; here and beyond any way.

Never it would be too late, to shed tinsel of worldly possessions,

Getting rid of the distracting obsessions:

Why seek evanescent, beguiling pleasures,

And happiness masquerade;

Which lies not in objects, to measure;
But in good deeds, let these proliferate:

Qualifying next slot; will be the only baggage in the last Journey on board:

Rest all, lock, stock and barrel, will be on hold.

10.

"Poetry" — English/Urdu

My romance with Urdu poetry began,
Listening to Ghalib's couplets,
recited characteristically, by my father;
Having not formally learnt the language,
yet I would try to gather,
To the best of my ability, being an ardent fan.

There comes upon the scene, my morning walk friend[1]*,*
a storehouse of poetry:
My love for the newfound hobby, manifold grew;
Opening new prospects, earlier in my possession were few:
Writing down in Roman, learning, remembering and
reciting to friends, with gaiety.

From my visits to Delhi, few books of different
Urdu poets, I would always carry;
And over the years, built up a good collection in
my library, and feel merry.

Simultaneously, my love for English poetry too
came to the fore;

Though an inherited legacy to the core,
my intense urge to write, I hadn't felt before.

My expression, prose in poetry,
gradually was becoming a style;

Of my writing, I didn't realize,
for quite a while.

William Shakespeare's plays,
once I would hear from my father enjoying every bit;

Would regale me, going over and over again,
now for hours would keep me sit.

Before proceed I further,
mentioning the ancient epic poems,
I just can't ignore;

Like the Sumerian's epic of Gilgamesh[2] *,*
believed to be the oldest, of the 2100BC,
and then many more;

Like the Homer's famous Iliad and odyssey[3]
of 8th century BC of foundational Greek culture;

Like India's ancient Sanskrit poems of Vedic period,
come to the fore.

The Maharishi Valmiki's Ramayana[4],
in 200BC-200AD[5] composed;

With 24000 verses of the earlier epic phase,
and of later Hindu religious practices, to nurture.

And the longest poem ever written,
composed between 400BC-300AD[6],
the present Mahabharata[7];

With original edition of 24000 verses by
Rishi Vyas, called the Bharata Samhita;

Enlarged and then condensed to 1 Lakh Shlokas[8],
based on lays, ballads and traditions of the war, refined;
10 times the size of Iliad and Odyssey combined.

The ultimate of the Mahabharata,
the sacred Bhagwat Gita, the essence;

Of human life, relevant then,
now and for all times, hence.

Handing over to poetry, having given my brief,
I will let poetry now trace,
Its journey in its own words,
and at its pace;
In general, and in English/Urdu in particular,
across time and space.

What after all, abstract or absolute, am I?
Sought after by the thinking mind;

Aesthetic in essence, a literary marvel of its kind;
Stretching the human imagination, well nigh.

Beyond known realms, weaving the thoughts;
In forms and styles, laureate poets besought
Of the contemporary era, riding on the wings of time:
With skilful matrix of alliterations, metaphors and rhyme.

Like other languages the world over, my journey in
English literature;
Beginning 5th century AD, period Anglo-Saxon[9];
Anonymous initially, best known "Beowulf,"
"Seafarer ", few to mention;
In alliterative old English, unrhymed on religious
faith, tales of valour, it's main feature.

Then came the middle ages[10] (1066-1500),
language developing to some standard;
Though still alliterative, but with meters and rhymes;
In the verse lines, renaissance expanding
the scope and the trend:
Greek and Roman literature[11] proliferated in
Europe with secular beliefs, prime.

Geoffrey Chaucer[12] *(1340-1400), father of my English*
version, making me sublime;
During 16th century, Renaissance
Blossoming in full bloom;
With language cogent and rhythmic, and unfolding soon:
Was age of English drama, with Shakespeare,
Ben Jonson, great heroes of the time.

Breaking away gradually from Greek and
Roman influence;
Birth of English romanticism, Elizabethan period[13]*,*
with profundity of thought, philosophical in essence;
I was uplifted to excellence.

In early 17th century, a new school of thought,
ignoring meters and rhymes, evolved;
Relying on, facts and arguments, metaphysical poets[14] *were*
involved.

The age of John Milton also called Puritan,[15]
was close on the heels:
Regaining the grandeur of English verse,
on the time's wheels.

Famous for the Epics by Milton "Paradise lost"
and "Paradise regained"
In grand style, heroic verse, with classical
style maintained.

17th - 18th century, the neo-classical age[16];
Poets following the Roman classical,
Did not last long, as a new beginning did presage.

William Blake, William Wordsworth came on the stage
With lyrical ballads, there began a romantic age[17].
Keeping up the pace, P.B. Shelly,
John Keats and Lord Byron, men of stature;
Preferring common language, with imaginative skills,
were lovers of nature.

Follows the period (1832-1901), known as
Victorian[18], of prolific literary production;
Alfred Tennyson, Mathew Arnold, Thomas Hardy,
may I mention.
Proponents of religious and secular didacticism;
Period of Karl Marx's socialism,
and industrial revolution.

Carrying forward my journey, from the beginning of
the First World War, till the end,
A new trend evolved[19], a break away from the
traditional way;
Symbolism, expressionism, would descend:
T.S. Eliot, W.B. Yeats, and other laureates mentioned
earlier, make me immortal in the sway.

Last but not the least, poets of modern times[20],
go beyond the convention;
Seeing closely at the real life, neglecting rules,
I mentioned.
Of meters, stanza's, forms and styles;
Many would think of me, like modern paintings,
riot of colours and its guiles.

Within the wide spectrum, main categories[21]
come to my mind;
Lyrical sonnets, narrative and dramatic ballads
each one of its kind;
Though one may use the other, at times.

Many are my forms[22], like blank verse, free verse,
rhymed in various ways;
Blank verse, without a rhyme scheme,
but in consistent meter, usually iambic pentameter;
Like in Shakespeare's sonnets, and in some famous plays:
And free verse with no restraint,
on number of words, syllables, or meters.

Rhymed verse, an artistic way to stay;
To play with the words, similar sounding
without going astray,
From within the line and at the end, for a
good effect, not to go away.

Various are my structures and rhyming patterns[23];
Of line, meter, stanza length,
from a single couplet to 4 liner quatrain;
6 liner stanza, a sexain.
Also called a sestet, should it be the last six lines,
of the 14 line Italian or Petrarchan's.

An 8-liner poem called octave, first part of the Italian
sonnet of iambic pentameter, may I say;
With the most common rhyme scheme in, ABBA/ABBA.

The ultimate 14-line poem like a sonnet,
either a combination of octave and sestet;
Or like Shakespearean sonnets,
with rhyme scheme ABAB/CDCD/EFEF/GG,
in three quatrains and a couplet.

A unique model, of 281 sonnets, of Vikram Seth's;
Broadly following Shakespearean sonnet model,
of three quatrains and a closing couplet,
but with ABAB/CCDD/EFFE/ and GG,
in "Golden Gate".

Like English literature, my journey in
Urdu too has been enigmatic, to define.

The very word, derived from "ordu" (army) has given
English the word horde;

Developed from the local dialects around Delhi,
called Dehalvi[24] and more:
The Turkish, Arabic and Persian combined in the
13th-14th century[25], to today's Hindi and Urdu refined.

Prolific Amir Khusru[26], father of present
Hindi and Urdu, credited,
As first writer to popularize Hindavi,
as Dehalvi he referred;
From the spoken dialect Rekhta or Hindi,
commonly known Lashkari, was inherited.

To the word Urdu and the language,
the great Urdu poet Mir-Taqi-Mir, did refer;
Mushafi being the first to use,
in his first Divan free collection of poems he offered.

Starting my journey in India[27] in Deccan,
with Wali Deccanni taking off,
Along with Siraj Aurangabadi, on a glorious path;
With three major schools of Shayri,
in Deccan, Delhi and Lucknow, did I embark.

In the 18th and 19th century, Mir-Taqi-Mir,
Asadullah Ghalib, Mir Dard and Dag,
legends of their time;
Uplifting romantically me, with Ghazal to its
zenith, their parallel difficult to find.

Like English, in my Urdu version,
various styles and structures are maintained;

Ghazal singing, Qawalis and Mushairas
were common, the culture still remains.

Ghazal, an Arabic word, with the beloved in conversation;
Developing in 10th century A.D, from Persia.
A Ballad, a long poem in Urdu, in Persian or
Arabic presentation;
Narrating battles, glorifying Kings, with lot of inertia.

Ghazal with a multiple theme, originating in
India in 12th century,
under Islamic Sultanates, and courtesy Sufi mystics;
Proliferated here in Persian and later in Urdu,
with a zeal, and not optics.

With least 5 couplets, up to fifteen conventionally;
With a defined structure, opening
couplet called MATLA;
Setting the tone of the poem and the rhyme rationally:

Subsequent couplets follow the pattern, the last
verse with pen name of the poet, called MAQTA.

2nd line of each couplet also called Shair,
end with Radeef, a word or phrase;
Repeated throughout the poem, enhancing the
rhyme, tone and its grace.

Qafia is the pattern of the words that rhyme; Just before
Radeef, in the second line.

As in Ghalib's couplet[28] "Hazaron Khvahishen aisi,
ki har Khvaish pe dam nikle ;
Bahut nikle mere arman, lekin phir bhi kam nikle".
Qafia, the pattern of words that rhyme here are,
as "dam" and "Kam" falling before Radeef, as "nikle".

Nazm, another form, well organized, with a
central and single theme;
Rhymed or unrhymed verse, even in free verse of its kind.
Poet's of the 20th century, like Sahir Ludhianvi,
shining example of an open mind;
Along with ghazals and mesmerizing lyrics, enthralling
audiences, becoming Hindi cinema's mainstream.

In my long journey, there also came along
Qasida, a petition;

With opening verse of rhyming couplet, as in
Ghazal, with 50-80 lines;
Popular in Arabia, glorifying King's and noblemen,
a patron, in the situation;
As suggests the very definition.

Having described, my journey in English and Urdu,
its structures and styles;
Comparing the two, will be a beguiling guile.

Essentially, I am a product of human expression;
Of literary minds, who leave indelible impression.

The language, basically a medium, each one in
her own right;
Has potential, for intellectual minds, to
transcend the boundaries, beyond sight.
Unfair it would be, making distinctions,
elevating one and showing the other in poor light;
I leave it to the audiences, my lover's to have
personal choices, liking and preferences, to decide.

Taking the charge back, conclude I may;
To save poetry, the embarrassment to say,
what it would but like to say.

Monuments will crumble to dust, on the wings of
weary times[29]*;*
Yet in the public memory, remain impressions;
Etched deep, through powerful tools of poetic expression;
Immortalized by lover's, through rhythm and rhymes.

❑

[1]My morning walk friend I referred to, is Mr Sanjeev Dhar, Retired Sr. Divisional Manager, National Insurance Company, Jammu (J&K)

[2-4]From https://en.m.wikipedia.org accessed on 25.6.21

[5-6] from the chronology of the book "The difficulty of being good" by Gurcharan Das.

[7-8] From https://en.m.wikipedia. org accessed on 25.6.21

[9-20] From https://www.literaturemini.com under the caption "The brief history of English" accessed on 25.6.21

[21-22] From https://masterclass.com accessed on 25.6.21
[23] From https://en.m.wikipedia.org accessed on 25.6.21
[24-27] From https://www.rekhta.org on Urdu poetry, accessed on 25.6.21
[28] Meaning: Thousands of desires, tantalizing one and all; Many a wish have I realized: Yet I yearn for more. Urdu poetry and translation: From K.C. Kanda's book on Urdu Ghazals
[29] The expression, inspired by sonnet 55 of William Shakespeare.

11.

"My Debts"

My debts were many, how did I repay?
First and foremost, towards my loving parents,
because of whom, I saw the light of day;
Under whose benign care, I didn't go astray;
Steering through the vicissitudes of life,
their trust I didn't betray.

Did I do enough, my filial duties
and responsibilities, did I fulfil?
The answer is very clear, not in one life span, one can;
Reimburse, even with best efforts and intentions:
Parents' love, as vast as the universe,
with unflickering will;
Toiled they hard to make me a man of
substance, without any mention.

Next was towards my teachers, and alma mater;
Did I as a professional, bring glory
to the institution?
I did endeavour, yet I believe I could
have done more, if I be a fair evaluator.
Towards society, which gave me recognition;

Did take steps, to do my bit, yet fall short in
my own estimation.

Towards the mother earth, biodiversity
and its creatures;
I did fairly well, quintessentially being a
lover of nature; Yet stubborn are the obstacles,
between man and nature:
I wonder, I may have ended up, my cherished
image's caricature.

Towards my motherland, my debts were huge.
As an engineer, in national building, I did contribute;
To my best capability, yet wish I wouldn't
need to seek refuge;
In the hazards, to which the deficits attribute.

With some success, shortfalls quite a few;
Rather than allude,
To the restraints; wish without regrets
I could clear debts and my journey conclude.

Last but not the least, towards my own self,
what to me is a debt;
Could I bring out my best, transform and exalt myself;
Did endeavour, to connect with the universal self;
I yearn to fully surrender to the merciful Lord,
with divine appetite to whet.

❑

Inspired by Rabindranath Tagore's Gitanjali Poem- 28, Page- 26.

12.

"Music"

Before going into technical details;
Let me relate, an overview of my family's love,
for music and few tales.

Liking for music, has been as natural in our family,
as was towards poetry.
My father in his youth, playing on guitar;
I as a child, on mouth organ, and my sister,
in college on sitar:
We all would reverie on the Bollywood songs,
light and classical in entirety.

My brother's love for music, I still recall;
Listening to Binaca Geetmala every Wednesday,
sitting with the radio close by;
Not to miss select songs and the iconic host
Amin Sayani's voice which still enthralls.

Nothing remains stagnant, and Indian
music transformed too, by and by.

Common sight it is, in the weddings;
To see rock music on display;
exultant moments and dancing skills interplay,
Adding gaiety to the occasion, and colourful settings.

Prompted by the festive mood, and inviting music,
some do actively participate;
Take to the stage, dance to the beats; Some would just
show up for few steps, and take to their seats;
But still enjoy, clapping with gestures, even if not gyrate.

Music lovers, listening to the euphonic tunes for hours,
Yearning to remain in the blissful state, forever.

Gradually and subtly music becomes a way,
To stay in our lives and we realize:
Reflecting in our conduct and body language, I may say;
Replay at will, happy notes in daily chores, to be precise.

Watching Indian Idol show on TV;
And to see, young boys and girls, of talent astronomical;
Singing the wide range, from rock music to classical;
Triggering dormant instincts of music lovers,
to refresh with glee.

Music, the art of combining vocal or instrumental
sounds or both and;
To produce beauty of form, harmony and
expression of emotions[1].
There being music for everybody, rock, Jazz,
and of classical[2] *brand;*
Grand is the art to produce a composition,
With unity and continuity, tones or sounds in succession[3].

Vocal, instrumental or mechanical sounds
with rhythm, melody and harmony;
Like choral, piano and recorded with musical quality;
Music of verse of orchestrated words, in symphony;
Composing with ingenuity, continuity and agility.

Bollywood songs and Ghazals, dominating the
Indian music Industry,
Drawing lyrics largely from Urdu poetry;
With variations of Hindi and Urdu, even
Persian and lately;
Hinglish, mixture of Hindi and English, speak of modern
cinema's creativity.

In its long journey, music did proliferate,
in many other languages[4] *besides Hindustani;*
like Braj, Awadhi, Bhojpuri, Punjabi,
Bengali and Rajasthani.

Classical, the soul of Indian music,
whose roots lie in the Vedic literature,
Of Hinduism, and Natyashastra of Bharat Muni[5]*,*
a treatise on ancient Sanskrit theatre.
With two traditional elements Rag and Tal[6]
Raga, giving the artist, a palette to build
the melody, to enthral;
With the Tal, making the classical music,
ever pleasing to all.

To understand the Indian classical music, with its
melodic and emotional potential of different ragas,
Thinking of the octave, like the light spectrum[7] *and*
the musical notes, like colour schemes;
Is a metaphor to better visualize a raga, I mean.

Music has the power to connect,
with our moods and its variations,
With different sets of notes,
triggering different emotions;
Music, being lifelong commitment,
with single-minded devotion.

Adhering to rules, classical music ragas,
to a high pedestal belong:
Two of the best known bollywood songs[8]*;*
"Man tarpat Hari Darshan ko
Aaj-Raag Mal Kauns, the one;
And "O Duniya ke Rakhwale" –
Raag Darbari, the other;

Both of the popular movie "Baiju Bawra",
still fresh in our minds;
Leaving footprints, on the sands of time.

Each one, a masterpiece of the music,
with Director Naushad;
The lyricist Shakeel Badayuni and the singer
Mohammed Rafi, the trio above all;
Live in our hearts, of millions of Hindi film music fans,
including me, one and all.

Devotional music of the sufis[9] *has its own significance,*
Poets like Rumi, Hafiz, Bulleh Shah,
Amir Khusro, for all times having their relevance:
Singers like Ghulam Ali, Mehdi Hassan,
and Jagjit Singh, doing full justice to
Sufi thought and its continuance;
And Qawali singers like Nusrat fateh Ali Khan,
Rahat Fateh Ali Khan, Sabri Brothers and
Wadali Brothers seeking divine benevolence.

Yet undoubtedly, old hits and classical,
for the elderly like me;
Remains a fond choice, to the nostalgic music,
we listen to with glee.

❑

[1]Definition of music from Dictionary of Oxford Languages.
[2, 3] from Merriamwebster.com.
[4, 5, 6] https: // www.en.m.wikipedia.org
[7]https://raag- Hindustani.com
[8]https:// www.ragasphere.com
[9]https:// www.en.m.wikipedia.org

13.

"My Little Self"

As I venture to tread the cherished path
I thought, was a call of the benevolent lord;
To unshackle from the worldly tinsel,
present and past; And choose the divine path.

As I take a few steps, do I realize;
Some hidden force, pulling me back:
I wonder, whether lack of confidence,
wouldn't let my mission materialize;
Mocking me, forget this arduous journey
and better pack you off.

Lingered, looked around, and thought for a while;
Is it worldly glamour, surreptitiously playing
acts of guiling guile?
And my will buckling under its load;
What else does it import?
Throwing to the winds, my new goal post.

"My Little Self"

My tryst with divine voyage, abruptly ends;
When I see the shadow of my own little self by
my side, till I make amends.

Toil hard I need to, to rein in my little self;
To transcend the barriers, towards the all pervasive,
Brahman, "the universal self".

❑

Inspired by Poem No.-30, Page no.-28 of Gitanjali by Rabindranath Tagore.

14.

"Windfall" — A Trap

To struggle, to seek, a goal in your life;
Falter, stumble, many a time grumble, yet be in:
Bottlenecks will be many, in the stride;
Not to yield but strive, and battle you win.

Reach you your goal, working on a mission mode;
Moving on, valuing your money
coming along the hard way:
The pleasure, your success would beget,
with pride on board;
Beggaring description, satisfying to
the core, all the way.

Should by destiny's sway, riches land in your lap, anyway;
As a windfall or of legacy, your spirits
would soar high, and lucky star would shine:
Your lifestyle would change, what was sane
till yesterday, looks claptrap today;

"Windfall" — A Trap

Earlier you would spend, now you squander,
think you it's your time.

Alas! The glitter and glamour, for
too long, will not stay;
Easily acquired wealth will flee,
as fast as it came,
Draining your vaults, as well health,
your happiness will too go away:
In your heart of hearts, you wish
to be back to your frugal ways;
And to the lord you pray; let it be only
divine bonanza that comes your way;
Lest you again go astray.

15.

"Prasad"

On a visit to a temple, Gurudwara, or any shrine;
Offer you, respectful obeisance in a mood sublime.
Prasad you accept with blissful feelings,
difficult to define;
Leaving an ingrained impression in your mind.

Is it the pure air and water of the reverential place?
That gives it the flavour, or is it the religious fervour?
Or the ambience, that leaves its divine trace.

May be the spiritual vibes, within the precincts,
Of the holy place, trigger the inner instincts;
Deep within, yet in slumber, to unwind;
Which overwhelm the devotees all the time.

I further discern to appreciate better,
The feeling of pleasure that descends;
The moment you step in the place of
worship, making amends;

Disarming your vanity at the threshold,
who so ever you are, no matter.

As you perform Pooja, offer oblations,
do other rituals, worth your while;
Practically remain you, in an ecstatic state to behold:
Even thereafter, spiritual aura, you still hold;
Recharged before you get back to the monotony of life.

Taking the sacred subject further, mention of the
community kitchens, may I make;
Of Sikh Gurdwaras' well-stocked kitchens
serving free meals to one and all;
On a massive scale, function these with
absolute ease, I may recall:
My uptake of these "langars": superlative
effort it is, of service to humanity's sake.

Like "Kadah Prasad," served in
the Gurdwaras, beautifully maintained;
Their sanctity, the devoutness and faith sustains.

During the pandemic, not only in
India but across the globe;
The "langars" and the Sikh community's
devotion came to the fore:

"Oxygen-Langar" for the people gasping for
breath, remain in public memory stored;
What a trail blazing gesture! uplifting "Sikh-Sewa"
to enviable levels, all the more.

Divine impulses become yet more profound;
Undertaking pilgrimage, with intense desire laced;
Than visiting a place of worship in your native place.
Greater the effort, greater does the religious
fervour rebound.

As I recall my visits to holy Mata Vaishno Devi Ji;
Chanting with full vigour, on each step I would tread;
Jai Mata Di, rather than to sit and rest, move instead.
Goddess Mata's subtle presence, in the Trikuta Hills,
I could sense if not see.

Ever since the formation of the
"Mata Vaishno Devi Shrine Board";
Attracting more and more devotees,
with better facilities in place;
But for the pandemic period, record numbers throng
the holy place; have "Darshan" with grace;
Undertake the pilgrimage, carrying
Mata's blessings on board.

Prasad from the priests, and meals in the
"Bhojanalya" at Bhawan, no less;
The flavour sanctified by
the landscape and its holiness.

Likewise, my experience of visiting Shahdara Sharief,
the holy shrine;
During my service tenure at Rajouri[1], is still fresh in
my mind.

Perched on beautiful mountains, radiating Godliness;
Ziarat of Baba Ghulam Shah Badshah[2]
has mesmerizing saintliness.

After offering deferential reverence;
The community meals, to all visiting would be
served like "Prasad" in essence;
And still I recall the taste, leaving an
imprint of heavenly presence.

My experiences of visiting a church are not far behind.
Having had the opportunity, many a time;
To visit with my family, attending service with
music divine;
Quite often longingly plays in my mind.

All places of worship are manifestations of
God's munificence;
To bless the pure souls, seeking merciful almighty's
benevolence;

Irrespective of the individual's faith, in
the universal lord's realms, have equal relevance.

To my mind, the following couplets of the Urdu poet Anjum are quite relevant and signify the beauty of the pluralistic society of our great nation India:

Jahan dil kushi se jhuka mera;
Wahin sar bhi maine jhuka diya;
Mujhai Anjum is se garaz nahin;
Yeh aàzab hai yah sawaab hai.

Meaning: Where my heart happily bows in reverence, I bow my head all the same; I bother not Anjum (the poet); whether it's a boon or a bane.

❑

[1]Rajouri is a border district of Jammu province, of union territory of J&K (erstwhile J&K state)

[2]Ziarat Shahadra Sharief is 35 km north of Rajouri. Accessed website https://www.jktourism.jk.gov.in

16.

"Joy"

If I was a commodity, in the markets would I sell;
In bulk, would the wealthy buy me, put in their cellars;
At their beck and call, I would be, without any pell-mell.

Not content with hoarding, in my search people splurge;
Flaunt their wealth, host big parties,
truckloads of goods they buy;
On their looks and dress, spend fortunes,
with an uninhibited urge.
Transitory happiness, they may beget for
a while; and fly in the sky;
A fleeting sensation and then back to
the groove, in disdain they sigh.

To seek me, many would travel across the globe;
With their families and friends, book choicest resorts.
I don't challenge human nature, their ingenuity, their
choices, but do they probe?
The glitzy world's beguiling guile; while
I reside much closer, than what they sought;

With all my mutations and strains,
I do live in a contented heart.

It's deep inside; it's visceral, and secure;
It's a feeling subtler than the subtle, a state of mind.
Seek me through your actions, noble and pure.

Surrender to the Almighty, the universal lord,
dear and kind;
The transformation from an agitating mind;
To the ocean of tranquillity, you will find;
Leaving baggage of bane and tribulations behind.

Ecstatic and lasting, the feeling benign;
After all you would find, with an effort divine.

❑

17.

Old Age — A Boon or Bane

At an unearthly hour, at my door tapping,
With steely steps, you caught me napping;
An unwelcome guest, a messenger of my
twilight with all its trapping's:
Shaking me in my deep slumber, from my
fanciful world, sent me packing.

In my frail frame, you sought niche,
Robbing me of my emulate pride;
How I wish, from your intrusion I could hide:
My waning youth, now deprived.

You may in your wisdom say,
By your subtle ways, dropped hints;
You being on the way, I tended to betray,
My instincts, to the reality I didn't blink.

Slowly but grudgingly, I did realize,
Old age has but descended in my life;
May have taken me by surprise,
Graciously I have to, take it in my stride.

In hindsight, could I clasp my youth slipping away?
Could I hold the realms of fantasy, I wonder!
If that could be, aging would be kept at bay;
Man then would be immortal,
to the inevitable I have but to surrender.

Mistily I gaze into decades gone by,
The balmy days and starry nights
Riding high, with no regrets:
Facing trials and tribulations, with never a sigh.

Childhood, it's fun and frolic, racing,
Whisking, tumbling, and hobbling[1];
On the vales and dales, climbing trails;
To refresh the memories are many tales;

Of the youthful days, when life was at prime,
Of love, romance, of vernal verve;
Of desires and ambitions, to serve:
Taking along vicissitudes on the wings of times.

Could I put brakes, in the journey of age?
Could I in my make-believe world, thwart the next stage;
Only to my dismay, not to accept the ineluctable:
Why not accept the reality, it's not reversible.

Apprehensions, afflictions of the mind, setting at rest,
Changing tack as I track the new journey;
In my heart of hearts instead; new vistas I beget:
And longingly behold newfound assets;
Of plentiful hours, with no rush,
At ease with me and myself;
Satiating fond hobbies, without fuss:
Spending productively in my study, with plenty of books on the shelf.

Let not old age, become your nemesis,
But with pleasant demeanour and grace;
Replace carapace of your stubbornness by a benign face;
Let you be the dignified master, of your space.

Rather than unlace at this stage, your hard earned reputation;
Why not lace yourself, with your cherished attributes, and with finesse;
Exalt yourself to enviable heights, staring in your face:
At this phase of your life, is your self-evaluation.

Let harmonious notes flow from your lips,
People at large and your family would
listen to with attent ears;
As worthy as words of wisdom from seers;
To face the world's dilemmas' with your tips.

Making the best of, though unwelcome yet
precious chapter, above all measures,
Of our journey, nature bestows upon us;
To spend sunset years, in service to humanity,
above all treasures:
Recompensing for our failed opportunities,
availing thus.

Through philanthropic deeds, we sow
The seeds to connect, with the universal lord;
In our cherished dreams we ever sought;
Our impulses grow on the divine path, steady and slow.

The other course to face old age
is to fret and frown, bereft of sanity,
Rather than to own the new stage graciously;
Disown the reality in ignorance and vanity:
Concluding life's journey unceremoniously.

Not to forget an unpleasant reality,
with the materialistic world on the roll,
The old somehow get ignored;

To the new generation's dreams and goals;
Loneliness, neglect, insecurity grip the withered souls:
On their glory and self-esteem, take a toll.

Many left high and dry do wonder,
Their life's earnings towards upbringing of
their children, they did surrender;
Could they in their wiser moments presage?
Their journey ending up, in the homes for the old aged.

Yet, notwithstanding the malaise of the present age;
It's largely upon us, making our old age
a boon or a bane;
Bearing with the constraints, making all
stages of life bright in the bargain.

❑

[1]The expression in this line is from the poem "Goblin Market" by Christina Rossetti.

CHAPTER 2

"Human Traits"— A Reflection

1.

"Monsoons"

We always look forward to arrival of seasonal monsoons, to breathe easy, get respite from the blistering heat of May and June. It's a fond weather of one and all, farmers to top the list, to have a good harvest. Our legendary poets have done full justice, romanticizing with their imaginative skills, churning out enchanting lyrics, for the Bollywood movies of the yesteryears. Thc lcad stars shooting for the popular numbers, in the rain drenched ambience, would in enchanting styles, play to viewers' delight. I too can't remain aloof to the munificent nature's invitations, and not say a word, as the monsoon arrived:

Rain washed shrubs, bobbing up and down,
as if in a celebratory mode;
Pitter-patter of the rain drops,
playing musical notes.

Whiff of moisture laden zephyr,
tinkling in the ears, making the ambience bright;
Brushing past our heat ravaged faces,
sensing our plight.

Sheets after sheets of rain, skies offload,
with a sense of pride;
Quenching mother earth's thirst, soothing
our senses, to our heart's delight.

Transported to the yesteryears, vistas of incredible
countryside, service career offered;
Breath-taking lush green landscape,
and dense forests I recall;
Trekking the hills, meandering rivers
and cascading waterfalls,
Munificent and benevolent nature, proffered.

I have vivid reflection, of the overflowing water channels,
meadows, and mountains with majestic heights;
Babbling brooks, towering cliffs in full might;
if my memory serves me right.
Resting for a while, lying supine on the inviting
green slopes, relishing the spectacular sights.

Nature's indescribable beauty,
speaks more eloquent than words;
Pandemic times with endless leisure,
has made many think like Wordsworth.

Our revered legendary poets had their own perceptions and ways to glorify rains-"Barsaat":

Gungunati see koi raat bhi Aa jati hai,
Aap Aatay hein to barsaat bhi
Aa jati hai.

– Kateel Shifayi

Zindagi bhar nahin bhulaigi wo barsaat ki Raat,
Aik anjan hasina say mulakaat ki Raat.

– Shakeel Bhadayuni

Bhaitha hua toba ki to khair manaya kar,
Talti nahin yun Johar is desh ki barsatain.

– Mohammad Ali Johar

Pee to laita hun, magar peenai ki wo batain gayeen;
Wo jawani, wo siya masti, wo barsatein gayeen.

– Hafiz Jalandhari

❑

2.

"Temper"

Temper is essentially a person's state of mind, angry or calm, composed or rattled, jovial or malicious. I took fancy to dwell on this tricky, yet a significant aspect of a person's personality. It is as difficult to describe this peculiar trait of the human beings as easy it is, to pronounce this short word. Spread across a wide spectrum, one's personality is a conglomerate of attributes, traits, failings, deficiencies, which collectively make human nature. Temper is an offshoot, encompassing wide extremities in its ambit. Such as, from calm, composed and mellow to an irascible, petulant and pugnacious; from a stolid, taciturn and an introvert to loquacious, gregarious and an extrovert. Sky is the limit to cover the canvas of human mind, with all its manifestations.

Whereas good temper, inherited and nurtured with self-discipline, helps in connecting with the people, maintaining relationships within the family and the outside world, with dignity and aplomb. Bad temper on the other hand, creates conflicts, estrangement and hiatus, which many a time becomes difficult to bridge.

Conscious of the fact, that it's a vast subject of social dynamics, I in my limited scope, did venture into this area and described my random thoughts like this;

"Temper"

Temper, a vital symbol of identity,
can make or mar one's personality.
Handled wisely, nurtured painstakingly,
and is in reality,
A good servant, but a bad master;
A good possession, why lose it at anger's altar?

Seeds sown in life journey's womb of time
will bear fruit when in prime;
Good Sanskars, inheritance, upbringing,
righteous deeds will make your life sublime.

Good temper makes you popular,
and you are loved in society;
While a haughty individual, would harbour malice towards
others, with no qualms of propriety.

A cool temper, sanity and humility would prescribe;
But the smug and the snooty,
to vanity and arrogance subscribe.

Vainglory, with stealing steps would claw you in
its clutch[1]*, when and how, you would not know;*
By the time you know it to be such, it will be too
late and the damage will be steady and slow.

Once smitten by inflated ego, and the malaise;
Creating hiatus, with the loved one's and friends,
with its capricious ways.

For whom you once would go to any length,
for the relationship to fend;
People who mattered in your life,
you would never offend.

Reasons for the temper's abhorrent transformation
may be many, and prolonged;
Out of blue windfall, neo-rich syndrome,
name and fame coming your way for a song;
Whatever be it so, something goes terribly wrong.
A course correction, to redeem the lost ground,
you surely can, though the process
will again be tardy and long.

How the degraded temper and arrogance reflect,
there is no scope for any ingenuity;
Conflict, heated debates, bouts of anger,
overtaking compatibility;
Flamboyance, overtaking sobriety.

Once a suave pleasing personality, now
becoming snobbish and a bragger;
Once cheerful and affable to people's delight,
now riding high with a condescending swagger;

"Temper"

Demeanour, body language says it all,
more eloquent than the words, description it beggars.

High time, even if gone astray, in the rough and
tumble of life, to right the wrong;
To correct yourself, reach out; retrieve your
rightful realms where you belong;
Lest you balk and make the task difficult,
if it lasts too long.

Upon the heat and flame of distemper
Let's sprinkle patience[2]; and rein in temper.

Ghalib's couplets are even more lucid and forthright, to bring home the point I am trying to make:

Udhar bad-gumani hai;
Idhar yeh na-tawani hai.
Na pucha jayai unse;
Na bola jayai mujh say.
Sambal-nay dai mujhai;
Aai na- umeedi.
Kya kyamat hai, kay damnai khyalai yar;
Choota jayai hai mujh say.

Bad-gumani ; meaning arrogance;

Na-tawani; meaning lack of strength

❑

Adapted from my Facebook post of 5th November, 2020.

[1&2]From William Shakespeare's play "Hamlet"; Act 5 Scene 1 & Act 3 Scene 4.

3.

"Human Relationships" — Many a Time and Sometime

Picking up threads from my write-up on temper as a core issue, with all its ramifications, with an earnest desire to salvage an afflicted relationship, yet many a times and sometimes, things come to an impasse. Eventually it culminates into an abyss, leading to parting of ways as a better option than to bear the burden of a soured relationship. I may very humbly put forth below my views:

Try sincerely we should, to salvage a relationship;
And retrieve with all humility and sincerity,
even from a precipice
The bondage we once had and the companionship.

Alas, many a times, the chasm is too deep; bridging
becomes an ordeal, a difficult option;
Albeit with the best efforts, with absolute
acquiescence, with the very best of intentions.

And sometimes, even if efforts yield dividends;
So inured are the scars, right or wrong,
whose fault, becomes difficult to decide and defend.
With no love lost, no bonhomie, on the reunion
no rejoicing would descend;
Howsoever to the contrary, we may pretend.
Therefore let's be careful, our arrogance,
not to become a scourge, making us later to repent.

See what great Urdu poet Ahmad Faraz said on this tricky subject:

Bhool jayein to Aaj behtar hai ;
Silsilai qurb ke, judai ke.

Meaning: Better it would be to forget; The sequence of our meetings and separations.

Bujh chukin khwahishon ki kadeelein;
Lut chuke shahr Aashnai ke.

Meaning: Candles of desire have since extinguished; Cities of friendship plundered.

Bhool jayein ki jo hua so hua;
Bhool jayein ki hum mile the kabhi.

Meaning: Let bygones be bygones; Better to forget, if we ever met.

Aksar Auqat chahne par bhi;
Faslon mein kami nahin hoti.

Meaning: Many a time, even if we wish, distances can't be bridged.

Baz Auqat jane walon ki;
Vapsi se khushi nahin hoti.

Meaning: Sometime, the departed ones are hardly welcomed upon their return.

❑

Urdu poetry and translation, from the book "Selected Poetry of Ahmad Faraz" by M.H.Qureshi.

Adapted from my Facebook post of 25th November, 2020.

4.

"Beatific Smile"

What is that, which keeps me going?
On a project, came my way, whether by choice?
I don't know, but what I know, was an innate voice;
Seeds sown in the womb of time, sprouting
now and musings overflowing.

Lying dormant, triggered by solitude;
As if giving elocution to the mute,
stand I in gratitude;
To my friends for the nudge,
reluctance given way to commitment;
Towards my own self, besides many
admirers and their pursuance.

As I sit hours on end, many a times
thoughts vanish in the sands of time;
Yet leaving a trail, caught up sooner than later;
Picking up the stream, no lingering look behind.

My adulations to the human brain,
the master computer, a unique narrator.

My efforts would be of no consequence;
But for plentiful hours, the ambience's quiescence;
And the pleasure of a subtle understanding;

With my better half, bearing with me
and my writing sessions unending.

She remaining busy with her pursuits;
I with mine would stay;
Her aura and invigorating beatific smile;
Sets the tone of the day, keeping languor of summer away.
The days slip by, I have yet to travel many miles.

❑

5.

"Eureka Moment"

My R.O water filter's malfunctioning put me on edge;
Novice hands, service provider sent,
messed up with all their might;
Relentless was I and within my right.
The filter wouldn't fill enough to quench
my small family's thirst and we were uptight;
Meantime it was revealed, changing its membrane, was the
main issue, rest may keep aside.
Took up with the GM, his company's
credibility was on a ledge.

A soft-spoken, well-meaning officer though,
sounded helpless;
With the lockdown restrictions, good technician's
reluctance to attend came to the fore.
I kept on pursuing and he assuring, the issue would be
resolved, and the unit would function as before;
At long last, I get a call, introducing him as Sunny; a good
wait nonetheless.

The name sounded to me no less than Indian cinema's
macho hero Sunny Deol,
Reporting dot at the scheduled time
With his kit, quickly got on the job, put in his soul;
Practically dismantled the whole unit and reassembled,
changing membrane, pump, pipes, testing the
filter many times.

I watched, dazed at his expertise and skill;
To me it was as good as a Eureka moment in sight;
To see Eureka Forbes unit at speed fill.
I wondered to my heart's delight;
How in his deft hands, lay a company's prestige and
consumer's plight.

6.
"Changing Weathers and Moods"

This year's winter has been severe but short. Premature spring and orchards in full bloom, do not augur well for the environment and the fruits; yet bring cheer to the tourists visiting the hills.

Moods change with the changing seasons, year after year undergoing the same routine though, yet looking forward to new experiences. Winter used to be once a favourite season during youthful days, but now it's an ordeal to steer through unharmed, the bone chilling period, remaining loaded with the woollens. Yet remembering with nostalgia the decades gone by, when we would dress up in style; whereas it's now shielding yourself all the while. I yearn to describe, the dilemma in my style; with comforting couplets doing the rest:

On the heels of winter riding the wings of haste, spring
prematurely arriving, summer not far behind;
Breathing easy, bringing cheer and respite, harsh weather
to the elderly, had been short but unkind;
From the woollens, jackets and caps,
relieved from the daily grind.

Winter, a fond weather for the young, socializing at will,
enjoying to their heart's delight, in their prime;
But an ordeal for the elderly, the health parameters going
haywire, guarding against the chill, all the time.

Nostalgia of the yesteryears flash before my mind's eyes;
Dapper suits and trendy pullovers adorning the
youthful body, spirits would run high;
For a while, transporting me to the
world of fantasy, well nigh;
Though pricked by the emulate pride[1] *of the era gone by,*
sooner than later, I realize;
In the sunset years of life, why fret and sigh.

Be well clad, forget fashion, put on a cap and
guard the shrivelled frame, why?
The dignity and the grace, resplendence on the
age beaten face, will still keep alive.

Jigar Moradabadi's comforting couplets;

Kisi soorat namood-e-soz-e-pinhaani nahin jaati;
Bujha jaata hai dil, chehre ki taabaani nahin jaati.

Meaning: The inner vigour does show on the face;

Though the heart weakens, resplendence retains its grace.

Bulandi chaahieye insaan ki fitrat mein poshida;

Koi ho bhes lekin shaan-e-sultaani nahin jaati.

Meaning: The excellence needs to be innate;
Whatever the attire, the royal grace, you maintain.

❑

Adapted from my Facebook post of 4th March 2021.
Urdu poetry is from, K.C. Kanda's book "Urdu Ghazals" — An Anthology.
[1]This line is from William Shakespeare's play Hamlet

7.

"Change Tack"

You take umbrage to someone's casual, at times caustic remarks, consciously or unconsciously aimed at you or by insinuation. You analyse later your spontaneous response, regret in your "heart of hearts", and wonder if that could be avoided:

Many a time you take affront, to someone's
general or specific, sarcastic comments,

To which you react, on the spur of the moment;
your response too gets malevolent.

A trivial issue, leaving strains,
Spoiling relations nurtured over decades, in the bargain;
Getting better of you, brusque stance, you maintain;
Disturbed mind, not letting your better sense, to regain.

Having had an unsavoury day,
In your sober moment, if you let the tiff replay;
Your response may have been too aggressive,
realize you may;

As you analyse and rethink, could you
put your anger on stay?

May also be, the words uttered, though in bad taste,
were against his grain;

Possibly, you could also get it wrong; introspect
if you may, would not go in vain;

Something else, he may have meant, to what
you thought, it may not pertain.

I too have had, few such unpleasant spats,
repenting later, into which I did stray;
Resolving, from such avoidable situations to
be away; to it not to fall prey.

Learnt gradually, facing such awkward moments,
by changing tack
Of my mind; the way it reacts, let me keep track.
Not to take umbrage and ignore claptrap;
Laugh over silly comments, don't fall in the trap.

Coming out of the trying situation,
with dignity and aplomb;
Making the other person realize, placating
his vanity or naivety, on one hand;
On the other, the precious camaraderie you save,
make it all the more strong.

8.

"Meet to Part"

Multitudes you come across, in your life and forget.
Your memories on test, with good effort from the
crevices you may beget;
Leaving ephemeral, translucent impressions at the best.

There are some very special, with whom your
wavelength clicks;
With each passing day, bonhomie picks.

Yet destiny having other plans, shifting them
to distant shores;
A mirthful journey abruptly ending;
cherished camaraderie no more.

Nevertheless, the memories bring cheer in your daily grind;
The very reflection, replaying the happy moments,
on the canvas of times.

"Meet to Part"

The story would be incomplete without treading on,
lover's domain;
World of romanticism, philosophers
And poet's choice remains.

As we look back, peep into our youthful past,
and let it replay;
The days were too short; the joyous moments
would slip away.

Dazed was the ambience, blue was the sky;
Young were the spirits, emotions were high.

Yearned for the fleeting moments, to be on hold;
Alas! The world of fantasy couldn't withhold.

The Journey of infatuation would end,
leaving trails of evocations behind;
Real or a mirage of its kind;
Yet yonder memories of the fanciful days, to
recall you never mind.

A popular song of Hindi cinema of the decades gone by, complimenting the theme:

Jeevan ke safar mein rahi,
Milte hein bichar jane ko,
Aur reh jati hein yadein,
Tanhai mein tarpane ko.

❑

9.
"East or West, Home is the Best"

Bondage with family and a strong desire to meet siblings, children, particularly grand-children, is very natural. One travels even to distant shores, to meet loved ones. You spend good time and enjoy your holiday, besides having a pleasant change you besought. Yet home sickness would overwhelm you sooner than you thought. Let me give an expression to the dilemma, from my inquisitive mind I sought:

Prompted by strong desire, you plan your holiday,
To meet your siblings, children, settled far away.

Reunion with the family, always very pleasant;
Hugs, chats, anecdotes unending, what to mention:
Reminiscing on years gone by, relishing the present;
The grand-children, remaining the focus of attention.

Endless sessions, time remains on hold;
Partying, get-togethers, uplifting spirits to seventh heaven;
Enjoying every moment, remain you in a
blissful mood 24x7.
Infinite, for each other, the love you behold.

As your pleasurable holiday is on a roll,
the heart yearns for even more;
The excitement of family reunion, with delight galore:
Yet as my holiday extends beyond a month or so;
The excitement abates, the mind transporting
me back to my shores.

The euphoria does no more stay;
I wonder, what has come in my way.
I fathom into my mind's core;
To know more; what is that which brings me to this state;
What comes fore is the homesickness, getting
intense by the day.

I reason with my vacillating mind, spoiling
my holiday, the change how to define?
All my comforts, well taken care, everything is fine.
Spot comes the answer; it's your minds
psychological comfort level, which begets
A feeling more than physical, you being as of now bereft;
Of status of master of the house, no other
position it accepts.

Commanding the household, doing what
you wish at your will;
Your cozy bed you miss, which gives you natural thrill.

Change surely is, an essence of life;
Holidaying with the family, a matter of delight:
Yet, not to trivialize the adage, why put it on test?
East or West, home is the best.

Could there be a better opportune time,
than the corona times;
To appreciate it, when travel is on rest:
And safety it suggests; to be in your nest.

The theme, legendary poet Jigar Moradabadi, through his befitting couplet, would further attest:

Koi yeh keh de gulshan gulshan; Lakh balaayain, ik nasheman.

Meaning: All through the garden, let it be proclaimed; Nest is best, bliss or bane.

❑

The English translation of the Urdu couplet is from "Urdu Ghazals" — An Anthology, by K.C. Kanda.

10.
"Idle Hours"

How did I spend my idle hours in my life?
Quite often it comes to my mind.
Whether on some constructive activity, elevating and satisfying, of some kind;
Or wastefully riding high, on the crest of times,
At the altar of the glitter and glamour of youthful times.

Pertinent to know, where from we get the idle hours;
Whether genuine or stolen from the productive hours?

Some just thrust upon us, from nowhere would descend;
Like stuck-up at blocked highways, with hours on end.
At the Airport, courtesy delayed or connecting flights, with frayed nerves;
With the mobile phones generally, idle hours are well served.

Surely, like maintenance of machinery,
our body too needs idling and rest;
To perform at its best, its vigour remains on test;
To withstand the vagaries, of life's vicissitudes;
It needs an interlude, from our tiresome schedules.

Socializing, holidaying too is important for a
balanced life;
From the mundane, to strive for a change,
away from strife.

Yet when I, my own idle hours trace;
I realize, many fruitful hours in the garb of idle hours,
were laid waste:
Now in my twilight years, with productive hours;
can't replace;
In this domain there is no cut and paste.

There could be no better time, than the
one we are undergoing, to import;
The value of idle hours, notwithstanding the havoc wrought
on humanity.
Many including me making the best use of, with God's
grace and sanguinity;
To spend time productively, like to write, to which my
instincts would exhort.

"Idle Hours"

Pray, may time's pen[1] breathe life, in my barren rhyme[2];
In idle hours of the bonus hours, if not in prime;
Make my life purposeful, all the more in Covid times.

❑

1&2 – Drawing inspiration from William Shakespeare's sonnet 16

11.

"Trust"—Be Aware

From the seeds sown in the furrows of time;
How many seasons you toil to see me sprout:
In your scheme of things, to shine;
Seeing my realms proliferating, I do feel proud.

As you prosper, in your name and fame;
Glorious heights, you achieve and sustain:
A subtle balance, you maintain;
I, like your partner, exult in your prosperity, all the same.

In your long journey of life;
You make friends, with diligence:
Using me, build the bonds, and the relationships thrive;
Many times you stumble, yet weave the
threads with intelligence.

But why when everything's going hunky- dory
You go astray, and change the course?

On the wings of haste, lay waste your success story;
Whether wilfully or accidentally, ending in remorse.

But it shocks me, seeing you fritter away;
Your lifetime gains and my possession:
Like a compulsive gambler's obsession;
By your impulsive, avaricious, reckless ways.

In my hindsight, as a concession,
would I vouchsafe for you;
In the public eye, your dignity and my honour, to see;
Even in your falsehood, looked you to be true:
But Alas! By your deceitful oath, you lose me.

In your world of manipulation;
May you think, to yet buy back my grace;
As if, I was a commodity, in your perception.
Let you seek solace, in Dag's couplet,
to reminisce my trace.

Khatir se ya lihaz se, mein man to Ghaiya;
Jhuti Kasam se, Apka iman to gya.

Meaning: Through coaxing and pleading, I was made to yield,

But you too, by forswearing, lost your faith and creed.

❑

Translation of Urdu poetry, from K.C. Kanda's book titled "Urdu Ghazals"— An Anthology.

12.

"Mind's Aberrations"

For reasons known, yet at times unknown, despondency descends in our lives. Should it remain unchecked, it will gradually make a subtle entry in our thought process, seeking a niche. Putting this malaise of human mind, in my own words and style:

Why my state of mind, these days is on decline?
As if drifted away, from the path of happiness:
From the exuberant life, how of it, I made a mess;
May be a wild guess, yet I can't for sure define.

Endless hours on socializing, I would fervently spend;
Now sound no more than a waste, and
onerous sessions of no use:
Not to refuse impolitely to attend, yet on
some pretext myself I excuse;
Conscious within, how from a convivial
to a recluse, did I end.

Dawns upon me then, why not analyse;
What after all bothers me, where are the fault-lines?
Has something gone amiss; whether my set
goals fail to crystallize?

How come, I am going down the line, rather than make my life sublime,

Solace I seek in Jiggar Moradabadi's couplets, in my mind:

"Tabiat in Dinoun, baigana-yai-gham hoti jati hai;
Mere hisay ki goya har khushi, kam hoti jati hai"
"Wahi hai zindagi jiggar, yeh hal hai apna, ki jaisay
Zindagi, Zindagi se, kam hoti jati hai".

Appreciating life's moods, its nuances on one hand;
On the other, legendary poet's literary finesse, bringing
home the point.

Yet, conjectures aside, when I sit and relax for a while;
Listen to my own self deep within, away from strife:
I do get the answer; yes, de-clutter
the confused mind, take it light;
Philosophy of life, you may analytically analyse;
But transitory aberrations of the mind
don't overemphasize.

❑

13.

"Truthfulness"

Rarest of the rare human traits am I;
Obscured, not immured, and by my volition;
Lie I inured in the chosen genes, by conviction;
Protesting to any transgression, attempts I stymie.

Seeds sown, in the womb of noble souls;
I germinate in determined minds.
My task as high as a mountain, remain I firm in my goal;
Taking a lifetime to withstand, the test of times.

Laboriously earning my place, stay I focused on facts;
Neither to be stretched, nor dwarfed;
Lest I am diluted and warped:
Unlike falsehood, limitless and amenable to deceitful acts.

My antonyms, many a times try,
Masquerading me, I see the wearers falling flat;
Finally entrapped, and left high and dry;

In the public eye, defending the indefensible
with this and that.

"Truthfulness"

To get to know, and define the true worth of mine
You do find, human tales in the Holy Scriptures;
The truthful bearing with slings and arrows;
whips and scorns[1] *of times;*
Yet stick they to their ideals to emulate, leaving their
signatures behind.

Blessed are those, who adorn me and my prospects;
May be bereft of estates, yet remain in a
good state of health;
In society, occupy lofty heights and respects;
Undergo hardships without regrets,
sans glitter and wealth.

❑

[1]The expression in this line, is from William Shakespeare's play "Hamlet"
Inspired by Urdu poet Firaq Gorakhpuri's couplet:
Sach gate yah bharai, to sach na rahai; jhuth ki, koi intihah hi nahin.
Meaning: Truthfulness loses its identity, be it stretched or diluted; Limitless is untruthfulness.

14.

"Perfection"

A three syllable word, holding fort right in
the core, I stand;
To stress my entity, what I am.
In the renaissance of excellence, my journey began;
The challenges of times, to withstand.

I am like a treasure, by many sought;
My very name, as you pronounce, triggering
a feeling of superiority;
Deep in the recesses of your heart;
Yearn you for brilliance, dumping inferiority.

I abhor indolence, no less non-entity;
Having no place in my realms, where only the best reside;
In whom I take pride, and they make rapid strides:
Many crave for me, from their world of mediocrity.

"Perfection"

The desire to reach my domain, in essence;
Is innate, deeply intended, not pretended:
Toil you, to maintain the high standard;
Of ever demanding performance, in quintessence.

As I by-stand, yet trying to understand the discourse, and
my intellectual friends' reverence and
reaction, to perfection;
In my heart of hearts, address to them, with
contentions none, but with apprehensions.

So far so good, bask you may in your glory;
Yet in my wisdom, let me caution you as well;
Pitfalls are not far behind, as a sequel.
With targets soaring high, vulnerable remains
your success story.

You being on the roll, on your health will take a toll;
The leisure hours, you revelled once in, will now be few;
Your inquisitive mind, may seek realms anew;
You would wonder, your peace, who stole?

Take fancy for perfection, yet other facets of life,
not to disavow;
Don't put all your eggs in one basket and sigh:
Not to become a robot, but to a balanced
joyful life, you avow;
You will still enjoy both the worlds, well nigh.

❑

15.

"Friendship" — Be Aware

Lately do I observe, a changed person in you;
From the camaraderie you withdrew, without
a rhyme or reason;
Our decades old friendship, seeming
no better than of a season:
I am amazed, how in our relationship,
an abhorrent virus grew.

A cold response sans logic, you show;
Your estranged demeanour baffles me thus;
What after all went wrong, let me know;
To sow, seeds of hiatus, between us.

May I invoke consonance of our bond, to call upon?
To know what prevents you to greet; when we meet;
I am at a loss to assay, this animosity where from?
To make bonhomie of years, to retreat.

My heart yearns, the bond pure and sincere,
could I retrieve?
Should you drop a hint if any, of my offence:
How I wish, you in your sober moments give me a reprieve;
To afford a chance to me, of defense.

Languish I, in your displeasure[1]
Strife who would measure; of reasons unknown,
On the wings of tricky times, seeds of enmity sown:
Stand I to your scrutiny, at your pleasure.

Why can't you share your malaise?
What is afflicting you, why not narrate:
Should I be the cause, in your comprehension;
With remorse, I will express my regrets, to your
satisfaction.

If you be mistakenly afflicted and I be wronged;
Either way, with the clearing of air, and as I long;
Redeemed will be the friendship to cherished heights,
where it belonged.

But if you choose, in your sagacity,
neither of the options and suggestions;

Aggrieved parties will be not just me and you,
but more than we two:
You in your make-believe world, and I suffer
being deprived of options few;
Above all, dented will be the institution of friendship, at the
altar of false perceptions.

❑

[1]This expression is from Act 3, Scene 3, Page 3, of Shakespeare's play "Othello".

16.

"Deceitful Gestures"

Your beguiling gestures, glances and stares;
Your bewitching blitheful grin, in the public glare;

Disarming me and my sense, unwittingly for me was rare;
Though unaware, in the world of fancy was I ensnared.

Your lustrous eyes, would emblazon the ambience;
Weave by night and day[1], colours gay;
Deep in my heart, would stay;
An imagery to write a sonnet, in essence.

Besotted by your fake charms;
I believed you to be, an epitome of love and beauty born.

Perhaps, your fetching smiles and laughters
were to deride;
My gullible instincts, taking me for a ride.

Your assent to a romantic relationship, with grace
In place, your actions would display,
In my memory, longingly linger and replay;
Alas! That was not to be, love was disgraced.

It was for you fun, your guile would enthrall,
Me in my naivety, in my own esteem I fall;
A prey to the realms of beauty and conceit;
Before I could see the reality and deceit:
No better than duplicity, it turned out to be;
It was a sham, trickery, I couldn't foresee.

Inspired by Firaq Gorakhpuri's couplets:

Kuch ishare the, jinhein duniya samajh bhethai the hum;
Us niga-he-aashna ko, kya samajh bhethai the hum;
Rafta-rafta ghair apni hi nazar mein ho gayai;
Wah ree ghaflat, tujhai apna samajh bhaithai the hum.

Aashna: Friend, Lover

Ghaflat: Negligence; indifference

❑

[1]This line is from Alfred Lord Tennyson's poem "Lady of Shallot".

17.

"To My Muse"

To you I beseech, to breathe in my pen, a life new,
The unexplored trails let me view;
Unlock the bonanza; enrich my thoughts, anew;
Not in dribs and drabs, but in full stream, not few.

With life upended, pandemic's ghost still not away;
Than to go astray, better would be the way,
To come up, with something easy on the eye;
Than to fret, frown and sigh.

Sometimes I think, you may be preoccupied,
I don't know, if you intend to switch sides;
To your new admirers like me,
who pine for you, and you shy.

In naivety I think so, little realizing
your expanse and scope,
How can you, my muse, be hijacked or outsourced?

You being privy to my thoughts and emotions;
You being my source of inspiration.

Getting down to business with a focused mind,
Keeping compelling trammels if any, behind.
While I stitch my random thoughts;
Aware I am of the new realms, from you besought.

If I can, give eloquence to my words, to make
the reader's regale,
In these tumultuous times, I will feel humbled
in my mortal frame;
Admiration if any, shall be due to you,
so shall be your fame:
If anything due to me, shall only be my toil,
of whatever scale.

In your wisdom, should you ever fade away;
Your fragrance will still remain hence;
Like rose petals' scents; in essence;
In my poems, will stay.

❑

Inspired by sonnets 38 and 54 of William Shakespeare

18.

"Look Through"

You meet and greet, family and friends,
with glint in the eyes;

You hug and caress, toddlers and newborn, with all smiles:

With the growing up children, sometime lovingly,
at times with stern looks eye to eye;
To hedge them from the world's beguiling guile,
to shape their lives.

With someone in distress, with gloomy eyes, you empathize;
Your eyes more than words, speak well nigh:
Far more genuine than words, you sympathize,
Without eloquence, and frequent sighs.

The work culture, administrative heads devise;
To set the tone, in their own styles;
Narrative they emphasize, with firm and meaningful eyes;
To employees to deliver; and in their output take pride.

The lovebirds, for hours on end, looking
into each other's eyes;
Stymie any distraction, lost in their world of fantasy:
Romancing honeymoon couples, on the 7th heaven,
all the while;
Seek a niche in each other's lustrous eyes,
enjoying every bit of ecstasy.

Many a time, in a stand-off with the adversary,
we do recall;
our armies defending the borders, have been
eyeball to eyeball;
To thwart the enemy's deceitful gall.

Eyes, a powerful tool of human expression;
Innocent, benign or harsh, are its impressions;
Supplementing beatific smiles, and its wearers'
valuable possessions;
Not far behind are bewitching smiles
and glances, with insinuations.

Piercing eyes, with a sharp penetrating stare;
Furtive glances, from here and there;
You notice human traits, as you socialize;
Taking all kinds of smiles and stares, in the stride:
Yet there is one class, at odds and uncivilized.

"Look Through"

To settle some score, using God gifted eyes,
loathsome it is all the more;
Wilfully avoiding eye contact, and looking through
Someone, coming across and known to you;
Keeping them guessing, disconcerted
and humiliated, and yet on the toes.

What else does this, outlandish and dishonest eye, signify?
May be impudence, egotism to suggest;
Or some remorse, balking eye contact;
What is up the sleeves, who will verify?

People honest in conduct and without
any ambivalence upon, to ride;
Do look straight into other's eyes
Without inhibitions, with nothing to hide;
Indubitably are honourable and wise.
Let society be deprived of the baneful eye to deride;
Instead be ruled by the loving and benevolent,
under the Almighty's merciful eye.

❑

19.

"Heart Poor Me"

Of the size of a closed fist, a muscular vital organ I am,
Sitting pretty, from the centre slightly to left;
Beating nonstop 24 x 7, right in your chest;
From the embryonic stage, my Journey began[1].

Working in tandem, with your lungs and body cells,
The arteries, veins and capillaries, do I ensure;
Oxygenated blood, flowing into your body,
keeping life secure;
In a perfect mechanism, and everything works well[2].

As you grow, so do your needs, desires and goals,
Joyous and sorrowful moments, you undergo;
Like your buddy, meet your needs, small irritants I forego;
Bear I with challenges of life, and its bank and shoals[3].

Those of you, conscious who are, and lead a healthy life,
With regular exercise, balanced diet and
keep away from strife;

I too bask in their fitness and take pride;
To be in a mortal frame, who to tread a
cautions path do strive.

For the love stricken, a heartthrob, for the
failed romance a broken heart;
For the magnanimous and munificent, a big heart;
For the frugal and niggard, a small heart;
For the brave a steel heart, and for the meek a fickle heart;
My size and definition do change on the drop of a hat.

All your deeds, misdeeds and needs, you attribute to me,
How many, besides my vital role, do I have to play?
I am in deep sea;
Will anyone, once for all, make clear to me, it's my plea.

When I see endless references to me, I reverie;
And muse, whether my creation, besides
pumping blood and its circulation,
Would be a goal post of all human traits,
beyond my imagination;
Cherished domain of the poets, philosophers
and you all mortals ever.

I was so glad, Ghalib the great poet, pleading my cause,

In his couplet *"Dil hi to hai, na Sang-o-khist, Dard se bhar na aayai kyon"* saying so because;

Its heart after all, not brick or stone, why can't it swell with grief? Taking pity at my sight:

No end to my tribulations, things come to an impasse;
Of my possession, conflicting claims, who to decide?

Legendary poet Jigar Moradabadi, bringing forth the lover's plight,

"Ilahi ik dil hai, tu hi iska faisla kar de, woh apna dil batatay hein, hum apna dil samjhte hein",

Meaning: Oh lord, I beseech to you to decide; it's one heart after all; she claims to be hers, while I consider it my pride.

Thus, putting the case in the Almighty's court, keeping the two parties, to think and pause.

So far so good, but I take umbrage to your
slovenly habits and indolent ways.
Your avaricious and capricious instincts, I take upon myself
and you I vouchsafe;
Hoping you would mend your ways, and
keep me and you safe.

Besides your stressful life, to your gluttony too
I object, and to your food's choice;
Respect you should, your digestive system,
and listen to its voice.

Many a time, into your bosom, I would pour my thoughts[4]
Alas! I have my own ways, to convey;
Which you ignore and underplay;
Wish to my signals, you could give
credence in your thoughts.

Petrified and calcified by your indulgence,
intemperance, and under its sway;
From a healthy vibrant organ, a caricature
I become in a way;
Of myself, once in full glory, now a
victim of your recalcitrant ways.

Resultantly, as you kept on to balk,
To listen to sane voice, and to doctor's
advice to your peril;
Imperilling my circulatory system and the
arteries would be blocked:
To my chagrin, land you on a heart
surgeon's table, me under shock.

Excuse me, if you got it by birth, and I being too harsh,
Aware I am, of your constraints, of a congenital heart.

Nevertheless, to you all I pray, in all my humility,
To keep lifestyles healthy to the best of ability:
I being your part and parcel take liberty,
To put you on the cherished path, keeping safe me and you;
Why only few, let's traverse many miles anew.

❑

[1,2]Source: https://www.medicalnewstoday.com, accessed on 14.7.2021.
[3]Source: Line "bank and shoals" is from William Shakespeare's play Macbeth.
[4]Source: The line is from William Shakespeare's play King John.

20.

"Ornaments of Human Personality"

Face expression, smile and body language are powerful tools of one's personality supplementing the communicative skills. If you closely observe people in the motley crowds, in the social gatherings, it will amuse you besides helping in analysing the way they conduct themselves and exhibit their traits. Let me share my observations, notwithstanding the fact that someone else may be observing me too, the same way:

Whereas some would just peek or espy, as if gathering
something or getting a feel of the place;
Some would gawk or ogle at beautiful faces around,
mesmerized, exhibiting artificial grace.
Whereas some staid and solemn looking,
displaying stiff disposition with a wry grimace;
With austere looks, stony and vacuous stares
and poker face.
Yet surely in the motley crowds, would also be
intrinsically urbane, with composed facials in place.

A gorgeous smile, transcends the boundaries of expression and it's style;
Be it the Madhubala's bewitching smile, making many hearts flutter in delight;
Or be it a fetching smile, electrifying the ambience, making it bright.
While there are genuine grins and cheerful smiles;
Not far behind, are the derisive smirks and jibes.
High and mighty, hiding not their condescending smiles;
Accepting as their birth right, deferential smiles.

Yet some find so difficult to smile, though an attribute of emulate pride;
Wrestling with their saturnine features, and constipated expressions to hide.

Nonverbal communication, what we call body language, unique to one's culture;
In consonance, with multiple facial expressions and gestures;
Complimenting individually and collectively, are gait and body postures.

Blessed are the personable, who adorn the ornaments of human personality, leaving an imprint of its kind;
But the stiff and taut, with arrogance writ large, don't mind;
Defiling the ambience, leaving bad footprints behind.

Nevertheless, superior to any other form,
There is one body language, transcending
the boundaries of cultures and norms;
A soldier's march past or his swagger;
The adulation it arouses, the salutations it receives from
the grateful nation, description it beggars.

❑

21.

"An Extra Mile"

Going an extra mile, making special efforts to do or achieve what one cherishes, sounds as beautiful as are the results, of following this phrase in our day to day lives. Taking fancy for this topic; this is how I perceive it: and bring forth its nuances in my style:

The phrase "An Extra mile" sounds simple,
yet so meaningful;
More than ordinary, making efforts purposeful.
Setting your goals high, sloth you decry;
You slog and don't sigh.
You think big, your spirits soaring to the sky.

Negating half-hearted proclivities, harnessing your
energies, putting in your best; whatever the task,
you take it as if your prestige is on test.

No gainsaying, destiny plays its part, sometimes
with little effort, some people do gain;
Yet in the long run, you may lose for a while, but with
sustained hard work, you regain;

The citadel of your success story, you maintain.
Your diligence doesn't go waste, your reputation
catapults you, and at high level you stay;
Unless you go awry, from the defined path you astray.

Gradually, a man of conviction, you become in sum;
The resultant outcome, the cherished traits
enter your blood stream;
Your words are not perfunctory, but what
you say you mean.
Respect you command in society, as a
person of substance.

Going beyond the boundaries of official work
or business interests, "An extra mile" approach
stands you in good stead,
As a responsible citizen, rather than a common
place attitude, with an outreach instead;
Of a good human being; a trust you beget.

The difference to the discerning minds is visible,
not to visualize;
Between those, who with the grief stricken sympathize or
empathize, though sounding alike.
Between those who make a casual offer, and those who
would genuinely proffer, travelling an extra mile;
Succour to the needy and distressed, without
thinking even for a while.

Not to purport, but with a purpose, an
extra mile if you trode;
Seek you in public memory, an honourable abode.

Leaving footprints on the sands of time,
Almighty's divine eye, not far behind;
A befitting couplet of Alma Iqbal would define.

Khudi Ko kar buland itna, ki Har taqdeer se pehle, khuda bande se khud puche, bata teri raza kya hai.

Meaning: Elevate yourself to such a level, that God will himself reach out to you, to know what you desire.

❑

22.
"Perception"

As complex I am, as simple I sound to be;
What you hear, become aware, and not just see;
But your receptiveness, and your discretion to see;
What you want to see is what defines me.

I appear, disappear like a stage play;
In your superficial memories, briefly stay;
Yet eventful events, unlike the daily grind;
Seek my niche, in your sub-conscious mind.

Your conduct, speech and actions beget me;
Giving you a persona, likeable or otherwise;
Subject to perceiver's judgment, gullible or wise.
Stand you in scrutiny, taking with a pinch of salt or glee.

Many a time your bonafide acts, fail to stand in good stead;
Get beset by your detractors, by their malicious acts.

Their hubris and mendacity, who would see,
In deceitful times, maligning your reputation
and falsifying me.

There are a lucky few, who get me right fortuitously;
With little effort, in the same environment:
Whereas many slog, to get me graciously.
All types nonetheless, jostle and yearn for me,
to be benevolent.

You deal with family and friends, in your own way;
In your wisdom, from the trodden path, not to go astray;
Yet at times, your judgment may betray;
To the unpredictable me, you fall prey.

Become I, all the more worthy, in the general domain.
The administrators, leaders, remain vulnerable to me;
Positive or negative, public discernment but to see;
Their delivery, actions, truthfulness, to sustain.

More seasoned than the seasons, may be you;
From your lens only, don't view.
Other's uptake, may not match with your take,
what you see;
Good would be a course correction, in the right
perspective, let you and me be.

❑

23.

"Maidens' Song"

Wandered I alone, over the vales and dales
Feasting my eyes on the enchanting landscape;
Away from madding crowds, a good escape.

Came across maidens working in the fields
In a chorus dancing with the breeze;
Swirling in colourful headgear:
As I passed by, their tuneful song I could hear;
The melody resonating the ambience,
My pace too became rhythmic, in sequence.

Bending over sickles, with a harvester's job at hand
In a style neat and grand;
Would they cut and collect the grain:
At ease with no strain.
Completing the task, with finesse;
A captivating sight it was, I was amazed.

As I traversed new valleys and clambered slopes
Countryside jaunts to me offered;
My trekking instincts to me proffered:
Capturing new vistas, with new hopes.

Yet beyond the scope of my imagination,
is the decades old;
Maidens' song, in my mind I still hold.

❑

Inspired by William Wordsworth's poems, "The solitary reaper" and "I wandered lonely as a cloud".

24.
How I Wish

It disturbs me, when I hear and see,
Sanity drowned in cacophony, of puerile public discourse;
One- upmanship, rather than to stay on course:
Falling prey to, without remorse, serving vanity with glee.

Whose purpose do the wasted hours serve?
High decibel eloquence with questionable verve;
Leaving the listener, common man, perturbed,
Wondering whether civilized society's domain being curbed.

How I wish, while dissenting voices and debates, remain alive,
Yet we strive, to keep our outpouring's style:
Tone and tenor, within decency and without wiles;
To let our great nation's, time tested value system survive.

Hordes of invaders, centuries of foreign rule, took we in the stride;

Influenced though, yet our culture survived:

We do take pride of, and bask in delight.

Should we throw to the winds our rich legacy, and ourselves disgrace?

To win points, unmindful of the stakes:

Our abhorrent acts would leave behind, to trace.

Let's not cross the red lines, let us not be in a race.

How I wish, our compulsive instincts we restrain,

With profound sanguinity and sagacity we sustain;

Peace at all levels in the society, equanimity and the balance we maintain.

❑

25.

Me and My Curiosity

Curiosity to know more, so far ignored
To satiate my instincts, keep me on toes.

Appetite unabating, new palate resurging
My restless mind, urging me to go beyond;
Traverse the untrodden miles, with my muse hand-in-hand
The cherished realms eluding me, now emerging.

With each passing day, the burden I bear,
My inner-self yearns to hear;
The vibes of the mysteries of life;
Unfathomed, beyond the mundane and its guiles.

Leaving the tinsel of the deceptive world behind;
Distancing from its sway, try I may,
On the calm pond of life, away from strife, I pray;
Put all my efforts, to seek the divine display.

Enervated though, in my dividend years,
Yet vital faculties do me the favour;
To savour the words of wisdom of seers
Toil I hard, to retain the newfound treasure.

❑

CHAPTER 3

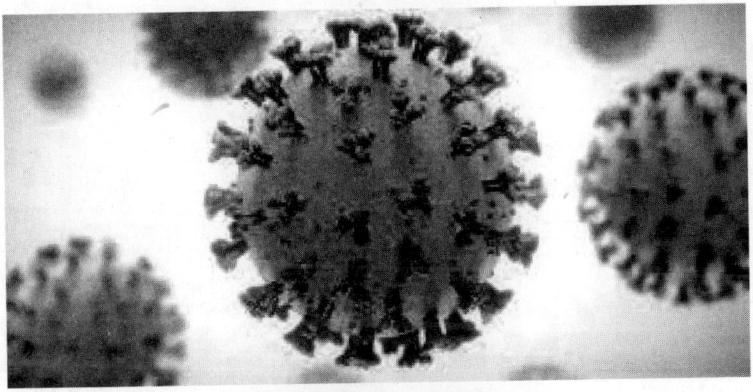

"COVID -19"— ITS JOURNEY AND OUTFALL

1.

"Glimpses of Biodiversity" — Homo-sapiens's Sensibilities on Test

We had a glimpse of biodiversity and nature's spectacular display, during the national lockdown early on, when human activity had come to a grinding halt. Let's have a review of the unfolding events thereafter:

What unfolded before us, with the human activity at rest;
Nature opened the cherished vistas, right at our doorsteps.
With factories shut, vehicles grounded,
social distancing on test;
Fresh air, redeemed and rejuvenated nature
was at its very best.

Irksome at times yet endurable, the lockdown
did teach us to sit for a while;
Giving a short shrift to the mundane and humdrum of life:
Distant stars visible with the sky clear;
Roaming on the expressways were Neelgais and deer.

Birds of all hues and colours, big and
small never seen before;
Big adorning the skies, little one's landing in
our gardens, bringing happiness galore:
Their chirping breaking the solitude;
Enlivening the ambience, complimenting quietude.

Basking in the placidity, relishing the serenity, yet with a
lurking fear not far away;
The deadly virus, longer than we think, may stay.

70 days of lockdown was followed by unlocking to retrieve the economy and livelihood, and save human lives from hunger. But we kept our fingers crossed, not to fritter away the gains in containing the deadly virus on one hand, and to maintain nature's fragile eco-balance on the other.

Rebuilding the battered economy as we get along;
Nature's vulnerabilities we may again forget
and the eco-balance norms:
Though fully aware, the Covid's birth directly linked to
environmental degradation, in any form;
So be the resultant climate change,
unprecedented floods and storms.

Sans greed there is need to visualize a new world, by
sustainability and simplicity;
By a reunion between humans and nature,
with new sensibilities and equanimity.

Creating wetlands, wildlife habitats, making urban centers,
symbols of biodiversity;
On the environmentalists, town planners,
architects, engineering fraternity,
Lie a big responsibility; to save humanity
with their ability.

❑

Adapted from my Facebook post of 26th August 2020.

2.

"Transformation in our Lifestyles"

Cooped up in the house, rather than getting cranky, there was a good option to devote time to the fond hobbies as well to the newfound, during Corona times. How our lifestyles have transformed, an insight;

Clearly observed as it is, Covid-19 changing
our basic habits, has transformed our lives;
Frequent washing of hands, once thought to be a
disorder, having become a new life style:
Regular cleaning the surfaces, handles, latches and doors,
now a new norm in the cleanliness drive.

With a discernible change in food habits, and
from junk food to keep away;
Healthy, home cooked food and snacks a
preferred choice, for a long time may stay.

In our fight against Covid, to build immunity,
and fitness to sustain;

Our ancient medicinal systems left behind,
coming alive again:
Herbal tea of Tulsi, Cinnamon, black pepper,
ginger now a favourite drink of its kind;
Along with workouts, Pranayam and meditation,
training human minds.

The way we dress up, we communicate, and
our priorities too have all changed;
To the new realities, we need ourselves to train.

Socializing with do's and don'ts, with occasional nods,
feigning an attent ear, courtesy maintained;
Struggling to decipher the masked conversations
and the subject to which these pertain:
To your profound satisfaction, may you steer
through the onerous sessions without any strain;
Will not staying home be a better option? If from such
gatherings you have nothing to gain.

Mask, besides a safety shield against possible harm;
Becoming a signature accessory,
hiding human expressions;
In its heart of hearts, seeking respite from
sticking impressions;
The attention face once invited, shifting to
its styles and forms.

Dapper and handsome, swish and chic men howsoever
personable, face half hidden and with expressions none;
Their persona as good as of no consequence:
So would be the beatific, lissom, svelte and smart women,
howsoever comely and classy in essence;
Without gorgeous smiles, with no impressionable presence.

Yet bereft of expressions and smiles, with a smart
gait and right postures;
Body language doing its bit, recompensing
with right gestures.

Last but not the least, a spectacular cultural drift
worldwide, is on display;
"Namaste" instead of shaking hands and a hug,
for a long time is going to stay:
India's traditional customs and value systems,
becoming a safe and dignified way.

Supplementing my stray thoughts with the most befitting Urdu poetry:

Dr Bashir Badr's couplets:

Yuen hi besabab na phira karo;
Kayi Sham ghar raha karo;
Koi hath bhi na milayega, jo gale miloge tappak se,
yeh nayai mizaj ka shahr hai, Zara fasle se mila Karo.

Amitosh Pandit's couplets:

Bewaja ghar se nikalne ki zaroorat kya hai ;
Maut se Aankh milane ki zaroorat kya hai.
Muskarana kya be-adab hota hai ;
Be-sabab hath milane ki zaroorat kya hai ;
Log jab hath milate huyai, katratai hein ;
Aaisay rishton kay nibhane ki zaroorat kya hai.

❑

Adapted from my Facebook post of 4th September 2020.

3.

"Testing Times"— Human Relationships

As Covid numbers kept on rising and the peak was still ahead, we were in general and the elderly in particular, gripped by despondency and paranoia, amidst the prolonged lockdowns. Yet the adversity offered opportunities to pursue our hobbies, as well to introspect on our way of thinking, human relationship and its sensitivities. This is what my inquisitive mind had offered:

Amidst the prolonged lockdown and thereafter;
With restrictions in force, at grave risk to falter.

Despondency and paranoia gripped the human mind,
elderly more than others remain on edge;
Away, distanced from the loved ones, shaken within yet
clinging to the hopes ledge;
That normal time will return, our optimism to it hedged.

Surely health tips, workouts and meditation
sessions help a great deal to calm the nerves;
Gradually becoming a new lifestyle, a
good enduring purpose it serves.

Let's not fret and frown; negativity let's disown;
With hours on end at hand, our potential has grown;
Realms not transcended earlier, inviting us to own.

Let's pursue our hobbies and enjoy our renaissance;
To stay connected with the family and friends, life's essence:
Not physically though, yet video calls, virtual meetings,
becoming beleaguered life's sustenance;
A phone call, an assured and easy option, at all times
retaining its own relevance.

Last but not the least; let's reach out to the people who
once mattered in our lives;
Got lost in the transitions of the materialistic
world, for a while.
Let's give our emotions an expression; and
not to make preoccupations an alibi;
Lest we get estranged and have to say good bye.

The legendary poet Ghalib brought home this point, cautioning us not to fall prey to such proclivities, and do spare time out of our schedules with all its constraints, for those who matter in your life, beautifully as below :

Masroof rehnai ka andaz ,
tumhein tanha na kar de Ghalib ;
Rishtai fursat kay nahin, tawajo kai,
mohtaj hotay hein.

Meaning: Your preoccupations may not estrange you from your loved ones;

Relationships are nurtured by your attention, and not subject to your spare times.

❑

Adapted from my Facebook post of 21st September 2020.

4.

"Mental Barrier"

Despite early spring, this year's summer, in our hilly state
Has been mild, with frequent showers and dust storms;
Freak weather, overriding the normal, lately
becoming a norm.
Till almost mid-May, torrid heat at bay,
a new experience I may narrate.

As the temperature soared, so did the discomfort,
and the strains of the day.
Suddenly the annual servicing, of the air
conditioner came to fore besides;
On one hand was the urgent need, on the
other hesitancy deep inside,
Of letting in electricians during corona times;
my mind won't accept any way.

What after all is the dilemma? I think for a while;
Is my Ac "Touch me not" till serviced or is it
my mental barrier?

My apprehensions not misplaced, the workmen I would
allow in, could be infection carriers.
Why can't I try my hands, clean the filter, in my style.

There I go, take out the frame and the filter,
Within half an hour, washed thoroughly and reaffixed,
serviced AC did glitter.

Of course, from my children came the inspiration;
A mental barrier, which held me back,
broke on a good suggestion.

Nevertheless, but for the scary times and its limitations,
My admiration remains to the skilled technicians;
Who remain on our beck and call; provide service
to our satisfaction;
Toil they hard, without many aspirations.

May the almighty, rid humanity of this deadly
virus soon, with his benevolence;
Bring our upended lives back to normal,
with divine consonance;
Restore the livelihood of our large labour force, as a
consequence.

❑

5.

"Diwali" — During Corona Times

On the eve of Diwali, a mixed bag of joy and trepidations gripped the mind, unsure to what extent should festivities during corona times be, amidst fears of possible repercussions, should there be laxity in observance of safety protocol. Be that as it may, this is what I will like to say:

Diwali symbolizing, the spiritual victory of
light over darkness;
Victory of good over evil, knowledge over ignorance;
Seeking Lord Ram's, Ma Lakshmi's,
and Ganesh Ji's benevolence.

Let the festival of lights; bring peace and
happiness in our lives;
Let gaiety and fervour, give us a reprieve from the
unwelcome life styles;
Rid us from the ghost of Corona for a while.

Rejoice and exult we may but with caution,
Celebrate the pious festival with due precautions;
Lighting of Diyas, candles surely will
brighten up the ambience.

Festivals do offer a cornucopia of pleasures;
Yet even in good times, more so during Corona times,
Adhere we should to the safety measures.

Having had lot of fun Deepawali offered, yet there
remained a lurking fear deep inside.
With social distancing and safety norms,
even for a while set aside;
Fears of Corona's resurgence looming large,
our festive moods left aside;
To its dismay, our muddled mind knew not,
whether to lie low or keep the moods alive.

❑

Adapted from my Facebook posts of 14th and 16th November 2020.

6.

"Nation's Mood" — On the Eve of New Year

As we step into the New Year 2021, the nation's mood is a mixture of hope and despair, with Corona's ghost still looming large, not inclined to part so easily, even though our daily infections rate has dipped down to 20,000. In an otherwise apparently improved COVID-19 situation worldwide and vaccination having taken off, we hear the disturbing news of emerging of three new mutants in UK, South Africa and Denmark, triggering panic around the globe.

After UK became the first country to begin vaccinating its citizens, the emergence of a new strain of the Corona virus raised alarm, as there was a sharp increase in its highly contagious variant in southeast England and London. Much remains unknown about the mutated version of the virus called B.1.1.7 which is feared to be 70 percent more transmissible. Mutations in RNA viruses like SARS-cov-2 is common, but 20 plus mutations contained within this new strain or variant of COVID-19 is unprecedented. We in India have a challenging task ahead, because detection of mutations is done by gene sequencing, available at few laboratories in the country, as of now.

The good news however is that Pfizer and Moderna vaccines, already approved against the Coronavirus in US and UK, can easily be altered to match up to the changes in SARS-cov-2. The vaccine named Covishield, developed by Oxford University and AstraZeneca, having a tie up with Serum Institute of India is too expected to be approved shortly for vaccination. India has also been planning to roll out its own manufactured vaccine named Covaxin, developed by Bion-tech in collaboration with ICMR. There are at least 8 vaccine candidates at different stages of clinical trial. We have to keep our fingers crossed till we actually have approved more vaccines suitable for our country, with our limitations of cold chains, cost factor and other impediments.

After having given a brief update on the COVID-19 on the eve of new year, from what I could gather and understand from the media and newspapers, I take this opportunity to wish my dear friends and their families a happy, cheerful, new year 2021[1], in my own style to set the mood right:

Be it the Pfizer, Moderna or Oxford vaccine;
Be it the Sputnik or Indian made Covaxin.
Sound like elixir of the mythical times;
Retrieving us, from the demon Corona,
riding high on the cusp of times:
As if finding joy of heaven here on earth,
courtesy vaccine divine,
Uplifting the veil of gloom, bringing back happy times.

Hardly did we breathe easy, reprieve from prolonged pain;
There comes along Corona's deadlier new mutated strain;
A dampener on the festive mood again;
Even though, scientists and experts assure us, not unnecessarily to strain.

The vaccines, capable of updation, safety norms will be sustained;
But not to forget, physical distancing, personal hygiene, masks, still to remain;
Till aggressive vaccination is done, herd immunity achieved, let's not fritter away the gains.

More than anything else, let's keep our turbulent minds cool, rein-in its mutations and strains;
For petty pleasures and materialistic gains, we must not lose the bigger battle, in the bargain.

Allama Iqbal's couplet's give the inspiration to the scientists who have been quietly doing their job without any fanfare:

Sitaron ke agai jahan aur bhi hein;
Abhi ishq ke imtehan aur bhi hein.

Meaning: There are beyond the stars, other worlds existent;
There are in the trail of love, other trials persistent.

Tu shahi hai, parvaz hai kam tera;

Tere samne asman aur bhi hein.

Meaning: You are a falcon breed; flying is your creed;

There are many skies to soar, for you to be triumphant.

The translation of the couplets is from Khwaja Tariq Mahmood's book on Poetry of Allama Iqbal.

❑

Adapted from my Facebook post of 29th December, 2020.

[1]The year however proved to be catastrophic later, particularly the months of April and May. The unfolding events have been covered subsequently.

7.

"Launch of Vaccination"

It was so satisfying, the smooth manner in which the anti-COVID vaccination programme, got off all over the country on the 16th January 2021. It was a tepid start though, amidst initial glitches in the functioning of the COWIN App and doubts raised about the Covaxin, despite the Government's and many top doctors' assurances about its safety.

It was a well thought out strategy to begin the vaccination drive with the health workers, followed by front line workers to boost confidence among the masses. Even otherwise the nature of their duties needed their vaccination on priority. Covaxin's roll out along with Covishield did cause unease and reluctance to some extent. A good number of beneficiaries however have already received anti-corona shots countrywide, and momentum is picking up.

We must however guard against social media driven misinformation, distorting reality even though authorities were relieved that adverse reactions post vaccination were negligible. The government is quite aware of the fact that the prestige of the country is at stake. India is the hub, the biggest manufacturer of vaccines in the world and has already dispatched vaccines to neighbouring countries as a goodwill gesture, besides having cleared commercial exports to Brazil and Morocco. Above all, to set doubts if any at rest, our worthy PM too sought to dispel fears on safety and efficacy of the Indian vaccines, during a virtual interaction with the vaccine recipients, doctors and vaccinators at Varanasi. He clearly stated that what has been done is what the scientists suggested and let's have faith in them.

To salute our scientists, I have penned down few lines, trying my hands on Urdu poetry:

Jazb-e- be-ikhtiyari; Aziyat se nijat sataai;

Yeh khushion ki bahar, kahan se Aai ;

Hamare Science- Danon ki, mehnat rang laai.

Akhir covid-19 ki vaccine jo Aai.

Jazb-e-be-ikhtiyari: Feeling of helplessness

Aziyat: Anxiety

Nijat: Freedom; release.

❑

Adapted from my Facebook post of 23rd January, 2021.

8.

"Morning Walk" — In Covid Times

What a tumultuous year 2020 has been! As we look back and wonder how the year upturned our lives, transforming our lifestyles, stretching our resilience to the limits. Amongst many constraints Covid-19 brought upon us, confined within our homes during lockdowns, and for a long time thereafter unless very necessary, morning walk became the first casualty. Though we could exercise, do yoga or workouts but those who have been routinely going out for a walk, found themselves in a state of helplessness. Reluctantly many including me and those of my age group chose the option of keeping the routine alive, walking within our four walls, in our gardens, driveways or on roof terraces.

I am sharing the thoughts that flooded my mind, when I chose the option of my garden with lush green grass, beautiful flower beds all around, with etched memories of the nostalgic years with laughters still resounding, when my parents were there who adorned the ambience, now to be used for a walk! Yet in these trying times, accepting the reality, I too chose this option, and share with you esteemed readers, my initial nervousness and later experiences:

Morning walk in my garden, keeping fitness sustained;
Such an option, to the very mention of which,
I would once react with a refrain.
Reality dawned, giving it a trial, sooner
than later, confidence regained;
In the process, within the confines of my house,
was my daily routine maintained.

The very idea initially looked absurd, thinking
how would I myself and my gait handle;
Will I walk or lumber, will I amble or ramble?
In the restricted place, will I shamble?
Achieving my target 4km a day, outlandish it sounded.

Periphery of my garden, eventually becoming a walking
track, keeping a good pace;
Slowly and gradually, with my normal getting apace:
Satisfying my self-esteem, of a seasoned walker,
keeping the grain of grace;
Of sorts, blazed a trail, in the limited space.

Settling down to a new routine, letting my relaxed new
lifestyle take care;
Enjoying the wrestle, letting it be infinite pleasure of
walking anytime, anywhere.
Once was in public glare, now in my
little world, why compare?
Why not to enjoy, what is at my doorsteps
and safe, why split hairs?

Keep I in my groove spirits high, yet faces of
the morning walkers come alive;
Good morning, Namaskar, Sasrikal,
Adab resound before my mind's eyes.

From heaven's messengers arrived:

Birds of all hues and colours, landing in our garden, in
chorus saying don't feel deprived;
We will keep coming, give you company, till you
go astray again, and eco-balance you deride.
Accepting nature as our friend and guide;
At the sight of these resplendent birds, I delight.

❑

Adapted from my Facebook post of 7th February 2021.

9.

"2nd Wave"

In our battle against COVID-19, everything looked to be going fine in India, when the vaccination was launched on 16th January 2021. But noticeable was COVID fatigue and a sense of complacency among the people, lowering their guard, perhaps because of marginal cases per day at just 9000 as on February 8th 2021. The second wave, of an unexpected magnitude and severity, descended with vengeance. The case load per day, started rising sharply and the exponential trajectory continued unabated and peaked at 4.14 lakh cases by 7th May 2021, before it started declining fast. The two months of April and May were devastating, and the deadly virus played havoc.

When our scientists and doctors were grappling with the prevailing variants of concern like, the UK variant, the South African, the Brazilian and the Californian variant, a double mutant viral strain B.1.617.2 sub type of B.1.617 variant was detected in India, called Indian variant later renamed as Delta variant. It triggered the 2nd wave, much more virulent and transmissible than the first. In the month of May 2021 alone, 1.20 lakh people died of covid-19, compared to 4076 deaths in the same month last year. The vaccination with its initial hiccups, did pick up gradually, yet as on 27th May 2021, barely 3% of India's population stood fully vaccinated.

The hospitals were overwhelmed by the unprecedented deluge of patients, and their attendants were standing in long queues for oxygen cylinders, even though as per Government sources, the oxygen generation had been enhanced from 6000 MT per day in August 2020 to 9000 MT per day as on 21st May 2021, but it fell too short of the demand. The heart wrenching scenes and the TV visuals beaming pictures 24x7 are still fresh in our minds. What after all went wrong, a lot was said and is still being debated, yet the fact remains, that collectively we all were directly or indirectly responsible, notwithstanding the fact that the western countries, far more advanced than us having much superior health infrastructure did undergo similar traumatic experiences during the first wave, falling victim to the unpredictable deadly virus.

After updating the events of the tragic times, let me give my personal thoughts an outlet, in my style and form; as I write this on 3rd June 2021:

When all looked fine, and we were on cloud nine;
Safety norms thrown to the winds, social distancing,
who would define?
Forgetting paranoia, tribulations of the mind;
Partying at will, confinement leaving behind.

Baring it's fangs, at the recalcitrant multitudes;
The virus double strong, and hitting hard
questioning the relaxed attitudes.

What unfolded before us, was beyond the
scope of our imagination;
Catastrophe wrought of monumental proportions;
On the unprepared nation, to take on double mutation:
Queuing up, for Oxygen and ICU beds,
was deluge of patients.

Under the unprecedented load, health
infrastructure was crumbling;
Telecast 24x7, were the ghastly scenes, heart numbing.

Analyse should we, who did our glory stole?
Rationally with a balanced mind, society as a whole:
Huge gatherings, social, religious, political,
were on the roll;
Denting our image, besides devastation,
distracting us from our goal.

With an extraordinary effort, Government machinery
swung into action;
Setting up held up and new oxygen plants, with
stakeholders on board.
Procuring oxygen cylinders, concentrators,
on a mission mode;
Transporting to the needy states, on a mammoth scale,
especially to mention.

Besides, the lockdowns did break human chain,
tamed was 2nd Wave;
Though in our life times, the painful memories
will be difficult to be erased.
Keeping our fingers crossed, clouds of 3rd
wave looming large,
Vulnerable shall we be, to the unpredictable virus
again, if we lower our guard.

❑

Source of the statistical data and related information is from the Ministry of Health regularly released, and from the national newspapers.

10.

"Wilful Defaulters"

It amazes me seeing people throwing to the winds, barriers of restraint; yet again holidaying, without safety protocols, with no social distancing and without masks. Having been ravaged by the 2nd wave of the pandemic, how can we, so easily forget?

The case load did come down significantly to below 40,000 a day, from the peak of 4 lakh plus, by 7th June. But then rapidly rising R factor in some states with another mutant Delta plus, a subdivision of Delta variant which played havoc in India with 1.2 lakh people dying at the height of 2nd wave in the month of May alone out of 4.19 lakh total deaths due to COVID-19 as on 24th July 2021, is a matter of concern. The said variant has affected 100 countries world over. The dangers of 3rd wave are looming large, and we continue to behave irresponsibly, more so when only 7% of the population as of now has been fully vaccinated and herd immunity is still far away. I pen down few lines, to offload my trepidations praying in my heart of hearts, that the virus scales down its virulence, mutations, and save the humanity from further devastation:

There has been a lull and intervals of calm;
Presaging a raging storm:
The way, we let down our guard;
Holidaying, thronging the hill stations, without masks.

With no social distancing, in our bravado we bask;
Forgetting the disaster of the 2nd wave
before it would retard.

With Covid case and positivity rate falling;
Recovery rate improving to ninety-eight percent;
To revive the economy, on the Government,
becomes incumbent:
With easing of restrictions, responsibilities
too come calling.

But public places present ominous tidings,
Some adhering, many ignoring, safety norms;
Meeting each other with open arms, as
if life was back to normal and calm:
What we have gone through, do we need rewinding?

As we stumble, grumble, fumble and sigh;
It is time to introspect, why?
Is it something to do with our compulsive instincts,
to know yet defy;
To eat the forbidden fruit, and fall to its wiles.

"Wilful Defaulters"

A wilful default to overcome, do we strive?
Having undergone many transformations,
traversing many miles;
Shedding the stubborn proclivities, and
weaknesses of the impulsive mind.

Denying access to the virus, let's be aware, if we may:
Protect nose, mouth and eyes, our three gateways;
By masking, avoiding crowds, with good hygiene and
vaccinations, safe let's stay.

❑

Source of the statistical data and general information on the subject as below:

Ministry of Health, GOI's press releasees.

Article by K. Srinath Reddy, in Times of India of 25th June, 2021.

Article by Jagat Ram (Director PGI Chandigarh) and Rakesh Kochar (Professor Gastroenterology) in Tribune of 22nd July, 2021.

11.

"Birthday" — During Corona Times

Special occasions do bring cheer, in the mundane of uneventful life, during the restricted activities, of the kind we are passing through, for the past a year and a half. It was one such occasion for me on 2nd August being my birthday. Amidst the phone calls and flood of messages of greetings, my mind in consonance with my muse; was churning out thoughts. Let us see, in the exultant moments, what it was:

The delightful word, whose very mention
uplifts moods, birthday;
Reminds us of the auspicious day;
We see light of the day; looking forward to
year after year, to replay.

Birthdays in our lives, occupy a special place;
Become all the more pleasurable, in the
twilight years, adding to grace.

Memories etched deep, of childhood and of prime;
Reminding of the celebrations, cakes, songs and rhymes;
Longingly stay for a long time in the minds.

Like last year, amidst pandemic, my special day arrives;
In the muggy weather, with humidity at its worst;
It happened to be my birthday on 2nd of August.

Forgetting claggy heat, uplifting my spirits,
soaring to the skies;
Resounding happy notes, in the music of my life;
Sequestered within the four walls; for
self-safety and others all:
How this transformation; Took a while to realize.

With the children and family, video calls face to face;
A feeling of bond, corona times deprived;
looked to be revived.
Were the trying times over and had normalcy arrived?
The blitheful moments, as if in a race, kept up the pace.

Undoubtedly, the euphoric moments will after all recede;
But why should I allow the tedium to transgress?
Of my special day, and few days thereafter, make a mess.
Let it be at a slumbering pace; be not in race;
Let it follow, why sour my exultant hours.

❑

12.

"Watershed Moment" — In Covid Journey

Credit rating agency Moody's upgrade of India's rating from negative to stable was a mood elevator, signaling getting rid of the worst of pandemic induced economic slowdown. Thank God, after the catastrophic second wave which receded as fast as it had risen, the Indian economy has bounced back. Recovery after the traumatic April-June quarter is dramatic. Yet we have to work hard to maintain the current spurt in growth and let's hope, our revived economy will keep up its present trajectory.

This turnaround has been made possible by our overall smart handling of the pandemic but for the bad patch of the 2nd wave's onslaught, which shook us off guard to withstand its wrath, for which we were pilloried by the international media, out of proportions. Nevertheless we did withstand the challenge and collectively, the Government, our worthy scientists, doctors, frontline workers and the people by and large, steered through tough time, leaving the past behind.

With some hiccups initially, our vaccination drive has been making rapid strides, with an impressive average of 79 lakh jabs per day in the month of September. **India achieved the milestone of one billion vaccinations on October 21st 2021, with 75% of our adult population having received the first dose and over 31% fully vaccinated**. Though we have yet to travel a long journey, yet the possibility of achieving herd humanity in the next few months looks possible.

In the backdrop of these positive developments, there was good news of the conditional approval to Bharat Biotech's children covid vaccine, subject to the final approval by the Drugs Controller General of India (DCGI). With Zydus Cadilla's vaccine having already been cleared for children above 12, Covaxin covering the age group 2-18 if finally approved, the two together will give an appreciable impetus to the vaccination drive.

Having said that, we surely need to further bolster our health infrastructure, with all hands-on-deck. We can't afford to underestimate the coronavirus's menace, till it is lock, stock and barrel gone. We also have to fast track immunological research, to plan for booster shots to take care of the waning immunity. There is no second thought to the fact that strong, elaborate, well researched data will go a long way, to facilitate pending approvals, in short term to comprehensively tackle Covid-19, and in the long term for future exigencies, making best use of the present lull.

Having given the update, I may in my own way; from the core of my heart say:

The nation's mood, retrieved after all from low ebb;

To an optimistic trajectory, with economy bouncing back, at a good pace;

Restoring the country's dignity and grace, to the rightful place;

Jettisoning the transitory stigma and negative cobweb.

The catastrophic events, of Covid's virulence;

Fresh in our minds still;

Yet with deft handling, resilience and God's benevolence;

As of now, 3rd wave kept at bay, with determined will, not by run of the mill

No way tilting at windmills, the enemy is real and still on the fence:

When it will again take offence;

When we lower our guard hence;

With the festivities on, can we ignore its imminence?

With the vaccinations progressing fast;

Herd immunity within reach;

To my fellow citizen I beseech;

Bear with your fatigue, for long it will not last.

Happy times are ahead, as you will tread on the new year 2022;

Rejoice we will, one and all, me and you;

Few months more, let's keep our spirits under control, if not on hold;

This great nation's perseverance, and strength well known, let's behold.

By the time I wind up my musings, my worst fears come true; putting a dampener on the moods anew. Omicron (B.1.1.529) with 50 mutations, a new variant of concern since Delta variant appears, first detected in South Africa on November 9th, to betray the blur of delight in the air. Later many other countries like Israel, Hong Kong, UK came under its sway. As I conclude, I am aware India too may not be far away and let me further say:

Be that as it may;

New variant Omicron is on its way;

Stopping in the tracks, wishful happy days;

Nonetheless I do pray, to the Greek alphabets, not to stray:

Further into deceitful times, why don the mantle of a commodity on sale?

Why become a symbol of morbidities, human misery on humongous scale?

Rather than to bask in the glory of humanity's helplessness,

Why not retract; stick to your genre and shun pettiness:

Why not emulate the great civilization, why perambulate through humans' distress;

Why not become a bellwether of their wellness.

❑

Referred to:

1. Statistical data from website of Ministry of health GOI
2. Editorial of Times of India Chandigarh, dated October 7th 2021.
3. Swaminathan S Anklesaria Aiyar's article of October 10th 2021, in Times of India Chandigarh.
4. Editorial of Times of India Chandigarh, dated 14th October, 2021.
5. Editorial of The Tribune, dated 14th October, 2021.
6. Article in daily Tribune of 26th October 2021, by Jagat Ram, Director PGI Chandigarh, and Rakesh Kochhar , Professor PGI Chandigarh.
7. Article in daily Tribune, dated 30th November 2021, by Chandrakant Lahariya.